FINANCIAL ACCOUNTING

Multiple Choice Questions and Answers

———————

Toye Adelaja

(BASIC FINANCIAL ACCOUNTING)
Copyright © 2015 by (Toye Adelaja)

ISBN-13 : 978 - 1519790996

Table of Contents

Introduction

It has been discovered that multi-choice questions have become integral parts of all financial accounting examinations in the world nowadays. This book includes many multi-choice questions and answers on each accounting topic. The book is designed and prepared for candidates preparing for financial accounting examinations.

It is very useful for students in high schools/secondary schools and tertiary institutions who want to know the rudiments of financial accounting.

The book contains various questions on each topic in financial accounting. Answers and explanations are also provided in the book.

Business professionals and other people who are interested in acquiring accounting knowledge will also find the book beneficial.

CHAPTER 1

Double Entry Bookkeeping /Accounting Equation

1. Which of the following is wrongly classified?

    A. Warehouse, account receivable, and loan to B. Black
    B. Mortgage of office building, inventory, and computers
    C. Warehouse, Machinery and Loan to B. Black
    D. Loan from bank, account payable and bank overdraft

2. C. Palic is setting up a business. $5,000 is deposited into his bank account. Out of this amount, $650 is borrowed from friends while the remaining balance is his personal money. Calculate the total asset.

    A. $4,450
    B. $650
    C. $5,000
    D. $4,350

3. Mr. Stone started business with $1,900 on February 1, 2012. He made a net loss of $60 at the end of the year. How much is his capital at the beginning of the year 2013?
    A. $1,900
    B. $1,840
    C. $1,960
    D. $2,060

4. Miss Eunice started a business with $2,500 on January, 2010. She earned a net profit of $1,019 at the end of the year, 2010. How much will her capital be at January 1, 2011?
    A. $1,019
    B. $1,901
    C. $2,500
    D. $3,519

5. A payment of an expense---------- assets

A. devalues
B. increases
C. reduces
D. change

6. Payment of accounts payable --------

    A. increases assets and reduces liabilities
    B. increase assets and increases liabilities
    C. decreases assets and decreases liabilities
    D. decrease liability and equate asset

7. What effect will an increase in capital have on assets?

    A. increase assets
    B. decrease assets
    C. no effect
    D. equate asset

8. The basic accounting equation is -----

    A. capital + asset = liability
    B. capital = liability + asset
    C. capital = liability + asset
    D. asset = capital + liability

9. Capital decreases if -------- decreases

    A. Revenue
    B. Expense
    C. Liability
    D. Drawings

10. Accounting equation can be best related to-------

    A. income
    B. assets
    C. principles of double entry book-keeping

D. nominal accounts

11. A business has the following items in it.

Building?
Cash $15,000
Plant & Machinery $300,000
Debtors $60,000
Owner's equity $500,000
Loan $250,000
Creditors $25,000

What is the value of the building?

    A. $500,000
    B. $775,0000
    C. $400,000
    D. $450,000

12. Which of the following is not a current asset?

    A. Inventory
    B. Short- term investment
    C. Cash at bank
    D. Bank overdraft

13. Which of the following is not an asset?

    A. Cash
    B. Cash at bank
    C. Account receivable
    D. Tax owed

14. A business has the following items in it.
Mortgage loan $40,000
Account payable $15,000
Account receivable $20,000
Machinery $200,000
Land and Building $520,000
Owner's equity?

What is the value of owner's equity?

A. $658,000
B. $688,000
C. $685,000
D. $720,000

15. A business entity has the following in it

Capital $65,000
Asset ?
Liability $15,000

What is the value of Asset?

A. $70,000
B. $65,000
C. $90,000
D. $80,000

16. An investment of additional cash into a business enterprise results in a/an

A. Increase in asset and increase in capital
B. Decrease in capital and increase in cash
C. Decrease in capital and increase in loan
D. Increase in capital and decrease in cash

17. One of the following stands as a separate item in the basic accounting equation.

A. Owners equity
B. Asset
C. Account receivable
D. Liability

18. Owner's equity has what type of balance?

A. Debit balance

B. Credit balance
C. Negative balance
D. Positive balance

19. Which of the following is an expanded accounting equation for a sole proprietorship?
   A. Assets = Capital + Liabilities
   B. Assets = Owner's capital+ Liabilities
   C. Assets = Liabilities + Owner's equity+ Revenue – Expenses – Owner's drawings
   D. Capital = Asset + Liability – Drawings

20. A change in any item of a basic accounting equation will have effect on how many items?
   A. Only three
   B. At least one
   C. Non of the items
   D. Four

21. Outstanding rent of $600 is paid by the proprietor. The effect on the balance sheet is ------
   A. Both asset and liability remain unchanged
   B. Liability is increased while the asset remain unchanged
   C. Capital Increased while liability decreased
   D. Liability increased while the asset decreased

22. Which of the following will be posted to the proprietor's capital accounts?
   A. Anticipated profit   B. Gross profit   C. Net profit   D. Net sales

23. Steven's capital at January 1, 1999 and December 31, 1999 were $80,000 and $110,000 respectively.
During the year he introduced additional capital of $13,500 and withdrew $8,500 for private use. What is his profit for the year ended January 31, 1999?
   A. $25,000 B.$30,000 C.$96,500 D. $93,500

24. The financial position of an enterprise at a particular time can be ascertained from

A. Statement of cash flow
B. Balance sheet
C. Profit and loss accounts
D. income statement

25. When a transaction causes an asset account to increase, there is an increase of equal amount in capital or
A. a decrease of equal amount in the owner's equity account
B. an increase of equal amount in a liability account
C. an increase of equal amount in another asset account
D. a decrease of equal amount in a liability account.

26. To realize an asset means to
A. use it as collateral
B. to turn it to cash
C. to remove it from the company
D. to evaluate it

27. Which of the following cannot be realized?
A. machinery   B. debtors   C. Goodwill   D. creditors

28. The golden rule of double entry principles states that----------

A. Debit and credit entry must be recorded and vice versa
B. For every debit entry there must be a corresponding credit entry, and for every credit entry there must be a corresponding debit entry.
C. Debit entry must be recorded before credit entry
D. Assets = Liabilities + Owner's equity

29. Double entry system is ------------

A. A reporting system
B. An accounting system
C. A recording system
D. Credit and debit entry system

30. How do you record cash invested in business by an entrepreneur, in a book of accounts

A. Debit investment account and credit cash account
B. Debit cash account and credit investment account
C. Debit cash account and credit capital account
D. Debit owner's equity and debit investment account

31. A proof of arithmetical accuracy of various posting in the ledger is a-------------

A. Financial statement
B. Balance sheet
C. Control account
D. Trial balance

32. If opening capital is $60,000 and closing capital is $58,500. What is the Net Profit or Loss?
A. Net profit $2,500
B. Net profit $1,500
C. Net loss $ 5,5500
D. Net loss $ 1,500

33. The concept of double entry book-keeping states that
A. First party receives and the second party gives
B. For every seller there is a buyer
C. every debit entry must have a corresponding credit entry, and every credit entry must have a corresponding debit entry.
D. Every transaction has double entry

34. Which of the following is odd?
A. Bank overdraft B. Machinery C. Preliminary expenses D. Goodwill

35. Which of the following is a fictitious asset?
A. Land and Building B. Plant and Machinery C. Preliminary expense D. Prepayment

36. Income received in advance is recorded in the balance sheet as a/an
A. Intangible Asset B. Goodwill C. Tangible Asset D. Current liability

37. The excess of current assets over current liabilities is
    A. Owners' equity   B. Shareholders' funds   C. a working
    capital D. Net Account payable is

38. When closing stock is overstated, it would increase
    A. Gross profit and reduce purchases
    B. Gross profit and reduces cost of sales
    C. Sales and reduces and increases purchases
    D. Purchases and reduce cost of sales

39. Which of the following will be excluded from the calculation
    of working capital?
    A. Inventory B. overdraft C. prepayment D. Furniture

40. Who invented double entry bookkeeping?
A. Roberto Pacioli B. Sabalele Rio   C. Steven Steigal   D. Luca
Pacioli

CHAPTER 2

SOURCE DOCUMENTS AND BOOKS OF ACCOUNTS

1. Sales Day Book is best described as
    A. containing suppliers' accounts
    B. part of double entry system
    C. containing credit sales
    D. containing customers' accounts

2. Sales accounts is extracted from
    A. Credit sales   B. cash sales   C. both cash and credit sales   D. Way bill

3. The Sales Day Book will show goods sold
    A. for cash   B. to customers   C. on credit D. to creditors

4. When a buyer returns damaged goods to the seller, the buyer receives a/an----
    A. Goods returned note
    B. Invoice
    C. Debit note
    D. Credit not

5. --------- is a document sent by a supplier to a customer whose invoice was undercast
    A. Credit Note B. Check C. Sales order D. Debit Note

6. Which of the following is not a book of original entry?
    A. Cash book B. Journal proper C. Sales journal D. Credit Note

7. Sales journal shows goods sold
    A. For cash B. on credit C. to competitors D. to retailers

8. In which of the following will trade discount be recorded?
    A. General Ledger B. Cash book C. Purchases day book D. invoice

9. Which of the following is not a book of prime entry?
   A. Sales Ledger B. Journal proper C. purchases day book D. cash book

10. Purchases day book is best described as
   A. containing customers' accounts
   B. a day book
   C. records of suppliers
   D. containing credit purchases

11. A credit balance of $5,000 in the petty cash book would mean that
   A. we have spent $5,000 less than we have received
   B. we have $5,000 cash in hand
   C. We have $5,000 cash surplus
   D. We have spent $5,000 more than we have received

12. Purchases journal can also be known as
   A. Purchases ledger   B. Purchases day book   C. Purchase account D. Accounts payable

13. A subsidiary record is a book
   A. of final entry
   B. of original entry
   C. of general ledger
   D. of debtors

14. Which of the following contains permanent record of all transactions?
   A. Journal B. Ledger C. Day book D. Books of prime entry

15. Which of the following accounts are treated in nominal ledger?
   I. Salary II. Discount received   III. Sales
A. I only B. II only C. I and II only D. I, II and III only

16. A machinery was bought on credit, the transaction will be entered by the customer first in
   A. Sales ledger B. Purchases journal C. Journal proper D. Return inward journal

17. Impersonal accounts is classified into Real and Nominal accounts. Which of the following includes real accounts?
   (I) Repair of machinery (II) machinery (III) electricity bill (IV) Land and building
   A. I and II only B. IV only C. II and IV only D. I,II,III and IV only

18. Cash discount is given for
   A. Being a regular customer
   B. Prompt payment
   C. Bulk purchases
   D. returns inward

19. A fund established for the payment of minor expenses is called
   A. Vote B. Petty cash C. Cash flow D. Reserve

20. Returns inward is overcast by $800 and discount received is undercast by $2,000.
   The effect of the errors is that, profit will be
   A. increased by $2,800
   B. decreased by $2,800
   C. increased by $1,200
   D. decreased by $1,200

21. The use of the folio in the ledger is for
   A. Referencing purposes
   B. Particulars of the transaction
   C. the account titles
   D. Only credit items

22. A fixed amount of money set aside for petty expenses is called...........
   A. an imprest receipt B. an imprest fund C. a float D. petty

23. When a buyer is undercharged, the supplier forwards a/an
   A. consignment invoice B. overcast note C. credit note D. debit note

24. The best way of correcting errors found in the ledger is through

A. Trial balance B. General ledger C. Journal proper D. Control accounts

25. Bola returned goods worth $2,500 to Timi. Bola should receive
A. A Debit Note B. A Credit Note C. returned inward journal D. an invoice

26. Which of the following is not a source document?
A. sales invoice B. credit note C. Check D. Journal proper

27. Which of the following is not a book of original entry?
A. Cash book B. Sales Journal C. Return outward day book D. General Journal

28. A systematic recording of financial transaction is called
A. Accounting B. Management C. Bookkeeping D. Budget

29. Which of the following is not contained in the journal?
A. Date of transaction B. Folio number of transaction C. Description of the transaction D. Address of customers

30. Which of the following is an evidence of goods supplied in good condition and number?
A. Purchase order B. Sales Order C. Goods Delivery Note D. Purchase invoice

31. The maximum level of cash held by a cashier under an imprest system is
A. a vote B. an advance C. a float D. petty

32. Books of accounts are opened by means of
A. Sales journal B. Purchases journal C. Principal Journal D. Sales day book

33. When both credit and debit entries of a transaction are posted in the same cash book, it is called
A. double entry B. dual entry C. contra entry D. compensating

34. The sum of money given to a petty cashier out of which small amount is spent is

A. a loan B. a vote C. a float D. a bonus

35. The total of the sales day book is entered on
 A. The credit side of the sales Account in the General Ledger
 B. The debit side of the sales day book
C. The credit side of the General Account in the Sales ledger
D. The debit side of the sales Account in the General Ledger

36. Credit Note issued by us will be entered in our
A. Sales accounts
B. Purchases accounts
C. Returns inwards journal
D. Returns outwards journal

37. The total of the Returns Outwards Journal is transferred to
A. Debit side of Returns Outwards Accounts
B. Credit side of the Return Inward Accounts
C. Credit side of the Returns Outwards Day Books
D. Credit side of the Returns Outwards Accounts

38. Which of the following accounting records are source documents?
A. Debit Note and Sales Journal
B. Sales Invoice and Cash Book
C. Sales Invoice and Credit Note
D. Journal and Ledger

39. Which of the following transactions is BEST recorded in the general journal?
A. Payment of rent with a check.
B. Payment of stock with cash
C. Purchase of a non-current asset on credit terms
D. Transfer of cash from head office to branch.

40. Linda, a ZAV's regular customer, owed $2,000 on account of computer bought.
If she sent in a check for $2,500, ZAV would send her a
A. credit note of $500   B. debit note of $500 C. receipt of $500 D. waybill of $500

41. The recipient whose name appears on check is
A. a banker B. a drawer C. a drawee D. a payee

42. Imprest account is a subsidiary of
A. General ledger B. Journal proper C. Sales journal D. Cash book

43. In what way is three column cash book different from two column cash book?
A. in cash column B. in bank column C. in discount columns D. Ledger folio

44. A subsidiary record is a book
A. containing the primary account.
C. of final entry.
D. of original entry.
E. found in the ledger.

45. Which ONE of the following, in a classified form, contains permanent records of all transactions?
A. Cash Book.
B. Sales Day Book.
C. Journal proper
D. Ledger.

46. Office equipment bought on credit would first be entered by the purchaser in the
A. Return inward journal
B. Purchase Day Book
C. Journal Proper
D. Sales Day Book

47. Suppliers' personal accounts are found in a
A. Sales day book B. Sales ledger C. Purchases Account D. Purchases Ledger

48. An allowance for doubtful debt is created
A. When debtors stop to be in business
B. To write off bad debt
C. To provide for possible bad debts
D. When debtors become bankrupt

49. Given a purchase invoice showing 5 items at $50,000 each less trade discount of 25% and cash discount of 10%, if paid within the credit period, your check would be made out for
    A. $187,500 B.$225,000 C. $168,750 D. $40,000

50. We originally sold 30 items at $24 each less 33 $1/3$ per cent trade discount. Our customer now returns 6 of them to us. What is the amount of credit note to be issued?
    A. $96 B. $69 C. $144 D. $48

CHAPTER 3

ACCOUNTING CONCEPTS AND CONVENTIONS, ACCOUNTING BASES, FINANCIAL STATEMENTS AND SOLE TRADER

1. The cash basis of accounting requires the recognition of revenue only when they are
   A. due B. earned C. paid D. received

2. The accounting concept which stipulates that money or goods taken from the business by the owner of the business for personal use should be treated as deductions from capital is
   A. Accrual B. dual C. Consistency D. Business entity

3. Assigning revenues to the accounting period in which goods were sold or services rendered and expenses incurred is known as
   A. passing of entries B. consistency convention
   C. matching concept D. adjusting for revenue

4. The accounting convention which states that 'profit must not be recognized until realized while all losses should be adequately provided for, is termed
   A. materiality B. objectivity
   C. consistency D. conservatism

5. When transactions are accounted for and presented according to their substance and financial reality and not according to their legal form, the principle applied is called
   A. Accrual concept B. Substance over form C. Objectivity D. Conservatism

6.The assumption that a business has a perpetual existence is recognized by
   A. accrual concept B. going concern concept C. dual aspect concept D. business entity concept

7. Accounting principle which states that for every debit entry, there must be a corresponding credit entry, and for every credit entry, there must be a corresponding debit entry is recognized by
A. matching concept B. accrual concept C. realization concept D. dual aspect concept

8. Which of the following is not an accounting convention?
   A. prudence B. conservatism C. materiality D. business entity

9. Which of the following accounting bases does not make allowance for depreciation?
   A. materiality B. cash basis C. commitment basis D. accrual basis

10. The practice of identifying with one constant approach where a number of approaches exist for solving an accounting problem is the convention of
   A. materiality B. consistency C. conservatism D. Money measurement

11. Which of the following concepts stipulates that accounting profit is the difference between revenue and expenses?

   A. Accrual concept B. Dual aspect concept
   C. Realization concept D. Historical concept.

12. All that financial information users need to know about a business entity is not disclosed in the financial statement. The concept is called
   A. consistency concept B. accrual concept C. monetary measurement concept D. prudence

13. Accrual concept states that
A. revenue should be realized when it is earned
B. costs should be recognized when the expenditure is paid
C. revenue should be recognized only when cash is paid
D. revenue should be recognized when it is earned

14. The accounting principle that is used to curtail the arbitrary action on the part of an accountant in a business entity is

A. subjectivity B. objectivity C. matching D. realization

15. .... states that a business will continue to be in operational existence indefinitely
    A. Prudence B. Going concern concept C. Accrual concept D. Realization concept

16. "Accountants do not count chickens before they are hatched". This is based on ......
    A. Materiality convention B. Accrual concept C. Prudence convention D. Going concern concept.

17. The assumption that a business affairs is different from the affairs of the owner of the business is
    A. Materiality convention B. Conservatism convention C. Prudence convention D. Business entity concept

18. Revenue is considered as earned immediately goods are transferred to customers in exchange for a valuable consideration. This assumption is called
    A. Accrual concept B. Dual aspect concept C. Realization concept D. Prudence convention

19. Assets are recorded at cost in the statement of financial position. This assumption is called.
    A. Historical cost concept B. Monetary measurement convention
    C. Materiality convention D. Conservatism convention

20. A plastic ruler purchased by a large scale manufacturing industry, is written off once to statement of comprehensive income. This is an assumption of
    A. Conservatism convention B. Realization concept C. Materiality convention
    D. Historical Cost convention

21. The fact that net profit is said to be the difference between "revenues and expenses" rather than difference between "cash receipts and expenditure incurred" is known as the.....................
A. Dual aspect concept B. Accrual concept C. Realization concept
D. Objectivity

22. Allowance made for bad and doubtful debts is an application of.....................................
A. Going concern concept   B. accrual concept   C. conservatism convention
D. monetary measurement

23. Which of the following is not an element of financial statement?
A. Statement of comprehensive income
B. Statement of cash flow
C. Statement of directors
D. Statement of financial position

24. Accounting information is used for
 A. Decision making   B. Information C. Estimate D. Analysis

25. Financial accounting information is used for
A. External use only   B. internal use only
C. Company's use   D. both internal and external use only

26. Users of subsidiary books of accounts are …………..
A. Financial Analysts
B. Risk Analysts.
C. Management Accountants.
D. Financial Accountants.

27. Which of the following is not a user of financial information?
A. investors   B. employees C. tax authority   D. charitable organizations

28. Which of the following functions is NOT the responsibility of an accountant?
A. co-ordinating the work of book-keeping staff.
B. preparing periodic financial statements for decision making.
C. Safeguarding and controlling the assets of an organization.
D. Taking vital decisions within the organization.

29. The term 'accounting period' is used to refer to the
A. Budget period, usually one year, relied on by the accountant
B. time span, usually one year covered by financial statement

C. a period within which debtors are expected to settle accounts
D. Period of time covered by tax computation

30. Creditors use financial information for the purpose of
A. improving sales of a company
B. controlling a company's affairs
C. investing in a company
D. assessing a company's liquidity and solvency

31. Which of the following uses of accounting information will not be suitable for an investor?
A. To determine potential earning power of a company
B. To evaluate the amount of debt owed by the company
C. To determine earning per share
D. To know the appropriate time for requesting for salary increment.

32. The main objective of accounting report is to provide information about
A. A company's shareholders   B. A business entity's management
C. The efficacy of non-current assets   D. A company's economic resources

Use the following information to answer question 33 to 36
The following were extracted from the books of Jeje Ltd. as at 31st December 2014.
Sales $180,000, purchases $168,000, return inward $1,600, opening stock $20,000, closing stock $48,800, carriage outwards $5,400, General expenses $12,000, carriage inwards $3,500, return outward $5,000, discount received $9,000 and discount allowed $2,500.

33. Calculate the Net sales for the period
A. $871,400 B. $178,400 C. $175,000 D. $180,000

34. What is the cost of sales?
A. $137,700 B. $700,137   C. $40,800 D. $186,500

35. What is the Gross profit?
A. $48,800 B. $49,700 C. $29,800 D. $40,700

36. Calculate the Net profit

A. $19,900   B. $29,800   C. $49,700   D. $25,000

37. One underlying principle of accounting that states the preparation of financial statement at a periodic interval of one year is called
A. realization concept   B. accrual concept   C. periodicity concept   D. materiality

38. Which of the following should not be considered as a reason for change of accounting policy?
   A. To conform to the requirement of relevant legislature
   B. To conform to the requirement of accounting standard
   C. When a change would result in a more appropriate presentation of transaction of a business entity.
   D. To maintain periodic evaluation of accounts

39. Which of the following is not regarded as an accounting convention in the preparation of financial statement?

   A. Materiality
   B. Prudence
   C. Conservatism
   D. Dual aspect

40. The traditional role of Accounting where management lays a report of performance before the owners of a business entity is regarded as
   A. Management function   B. Accountability   C. Stewardship   D. Auditing

CHAPTER 4

ADJUSTMENTS TO ACCOUNTS

Use the following information to answer question 1 – 3

A trader paid insurance premium of $2,500 for 15 months ended 31st May, 2008
He prepares accounts to 31st December.

1. How much out of the premium paid is chargeable to profit and loss accounts for the year ended 31st December, 2007?
   A. $2,004 B. $1,500 C. $ 835 D. $1,666.67

2. The amount carried forward in the balance sheet as at 31st December, 2007 is $......and termed as..........
   A. $458 ;Current liability B. $2,004; Current asset C. $833.33; Current asset   D. $1,169; Fixed asset

3. Mr. Babs owed office rent of $600 at the end of previous accounting year. During this year, he paid $6,000 on the account of rent, and $800 was still outstanding at the end of the current period. What is the amount that will be considered in the profit and loss account of the current year?
   A. $3,400 B. $6,200 C. $7,200 D. $800

4. Income received in advance is shown in the balance sheet as
   A. Current asset B. Current liability C. Non-Current Asset
   D. Income

5. Which of the following is one of the two steps for recording bad debt recovered?
   A. Credit sales accounts and debit cash account
   B. Debit receivable accounts and credit bad debt accounts
   C. Debit debtors account and credit sales accounts
   D. Credit cash accounts and debit sales accounts

6. What is the effect of a reduction in the provision for doubtful debt?
   - A. It increases Gross profit
   - B. It increases Net profit
   - C. It reduces Net profit
   - D. It makes Net profit to be constant

7. Which of the following is not true of capital expenditure?
   - i) It is fully consumed in one accounting period
   - ii) Extension of factory building
   - iii) Assets acquired for the purpose of generating income
   - A. i and ii only B. i only C. iii only D. ii only

8. Accounting terms used to described excess of current assets over current liability is
   - A. Capital reserve B. equity capital C. working capital D. share capital

9. When there is an allowance for doubtful debt, the accounting entries are debit
   - A. Debtors Accounts, credit allowance Accounts
   - B. Trading Accounts, credit debtors
   - C. Statement of comprehensive income, and credit Allowance for doubtful debts
   - D. Profit and loss account, credit creditors Accounts

Use the following information to answer question 10 - 13
      Mr. Femi, a farmer bought a tractor and 10 cutlasses for $450,000 and $850 respectively. He incurred the following expenses for the year ended 31st December,2012:

Wages	$69,000
Yam tuba	$11,000
Maize	$2,000

He received $4,900 from customers. The tractor was later sold for $250,000.

10. What is his capital expenditure?
      A. $81,000 B. $11,000 C. $450,850 D. $250,000

11. What is his Revenue Receipt?
A. $450,000 B. $4,900 C. $82,000 D. $250,000 E. $254,900

12. What is his Revenue Expenditure?
A. $250,000 B. $4,900 C. $850 D. $82,000

13. What is his capital receipt?
A. $ 250,000 B. $ 4,900 C. $ 82,000 D. $ 450,850

14. The term bad debt means debts
A. owed by customers B .owed by owner
C. that is bad   D. that cannot be collected

15. Purchases in accounting refer to goods bought for
A. resale B. repurchases C. owner's use D. repairs

16. Which of the following is the most liquid?
A. Stock B. Goodwill C. Income D. Cash at bank

17. Which of the following is a revenue receipt?
A. Revaluation of assets
B. Sales proceeds of fixed assets
C. Sales of finished goods
D. Income from sales of shares

Use the following information to answer question 18 and 19

Year to 31st December	Debtors after bad debts written off	Allowance for Doubtful debts
	$	$
1990	60,000	600
1991	65,000	650
1992	63,000	630

18. What was the treatment of allowance for doubtful debts in the statement of comprehensive income (Profit and Loss Account) for 1991?

A. Credit $630   B. Debit $630 C. Debit $650   D. Debit $50

19. In 1992, debtors figure will appear in the balance sheet as
A. $ 63,000 B. $ 65,000 C. $ 62,370   D. $ 63,630

20. Which of the following is an effect of reduction in provision for doubtful debts?
A. Decrease in net profit   B. Reduction in bad debt   C. Increase in net profit D. Increase in cash balance

21. Profit expressed as a percentage of selling price is called
A. Income   B. Profit mark-up   C. Profit mirgin   D. Profit margin

22. Profit expressed as a percentage of cost of goods sold is called
A. Profit margin   B. Profit/Cost   C. profit mark-up   D. profit margin

23. Joe bought goods worth $900 and sold it at a margin of 20% on selling price. How much did he sell the goods?
A. $ 125   B. $ 225   C. $ 625   D.$ 1,125

24. Services enjoyed in the past, but not yet paid is
A. Dual expenses   B. Accrued expenses   C. historical cost D. Delayed expenses

25. Which of the following is not a capital expenditure?
A. Extension of office building   B. Acquisition of machinery C. Purchase of computer for resale   D. Purchase of Motor Vehicle

26. Payment for service which is yet to be enjoyed is called
A. variable cost B. Accrued expenses   C. Future cost D. payment in advance

Use the following information to answer question 27 to 28.
The accounts receivable of a trading concern is $66,000. Out of this, 2% is irrecoverable;
5 percent of the balance is unlikely to be collected.

27. How much is the bad debt?

A. $1,230 B. $ 1,320 C. $1293 D. $3,300

28. What is the allowance for doubtful debt?

A. $3,234 B. $1,320 C. $3,300 D. $1,293

29. An allowance given to a customer by a supplier for prompt payment is called

    A. Discount received   B. trade discount C. cash discount D. rebate

30. When a proprietor of a business withdraws goods from the business for its own personal use, the accounting entries are

    A. Debit capital account and credit stock accounts

    B. Debit drawings accounts and credit purchases accounts

    C. Credit purchases accounts and debit sales accounts

    D. Debit capital accounts and credit drawings accounts

31. An example of capital gain

A. Share premium B. Share discount C. Bonus issue D. dividend

32. Which of the following will not be considered when estimating the amount of doubtful debts?
A. The age of the debts
B. The credit worthiness of some debtors
C. The choice of the debtor
D. Bankruptcy of a debtor

33. A business marks up its cost by 1/4. This means a gross profit in percentage of
A. 20% on selling price
B. 25% on total price
C. 20% on cost price

D. 25% on selling price

34. The cost price of a printer is $18,000 and the selling price is $24,000. The mark-up is
  A. 33 1/3 %   B. 25%   C. 50%   D. 66 2/3

Use the following information to answer questions 35 and 36.
Accounts Receivable as at 1/6/2013 is $300,450.
Accounts Receivable as at 31/5/2014 is $525,110.
Specific bad debts during the year are $41,000.
Allowance for bad and doubtful debts as at 1/6/2013 is $12,500.
The provision for bad and doubtful debts is maintained at a level of 5% of accounts receivables as at 31/5/2014.

35. What is the value of Accounts Receivables as at 31/5/2014 to be shown in the statement of financial position (balance sheet)?
A. $405,114.50
B. $551,904.50
C. $ 459,904.50
D. $ 285,101.50

36. What is the amount of allowance for bad and doubtful debts to be recorded in profit and loss accounts for the year ended 31 May 2014?
A. $14,405.00
B. $4,405.50
C. $11,505.50
D. $11,706

Use the following information to answer question 37 to 40.
The trial balance extracted from the books of Mr. Timi at December 31, 2006 included the following debit balances:

	$
Rent paid	2,000
Rates	1,500
Wages	72,500
Interest on loan	350

The following adjustments have to be made before the preparation of final accounts:

	31/12/2005	31/12/2006
	$	$
Rent outstanding	1,000	500
Rates paid in advance	500	600
Wages accrued	1,000	750
Interest on loan unpaid	1,200	1,400

37. Show the amount of rates that will be debited to the statement of comprehensive Income (profit and loss accounts) for the year ended 31st December, 2006.

A. $2,400   B. $6,500 C. $1,400   D. $1, 600

38. What is the amount of rent that will be debited to profit and loss account?

A. $2,500   B. $1,500   C. $1,000   D. $2,000

39. What is the amount of interest on loan that will be recorded in the statement of financial position (balance sheet) and as what?

A. $550; current asset   B. $1,400; current asset   C. $350;current liability   D. $1,400; current liability

40. Show amount of wages that will appear on the statement of comprehensive income, and statement of financial position respectively.

A. $72,250 ; $750   B. $72,500; $1,000   C. $72,850; $750   D. $750; $72,250

CHAPTER 5

BANK RECONCILIATION

1. Cash deposited into a bank account by a business entity appears as......... balance in the bank statement.
A. liability B. credit C. debit D. income

2. Bank reconciliation is done to harmonize balance as per bank statement sent by a bank with the ...... got by a business entity.
A. Cash book balance B. Petty cash book balance C. overdraft D. Ledgers

3. In bank reconciliation statement, deposit in transit is normally
A. Multiplied by bank balance
B. Deducted from bank balance
C. Added to adjusted cash book balance
D. Deducted from adjusted cash book balance

4. Bank reconciliation statement is ordinarily prepared by a/an .... of a business
A. Manager B. Cashier C. Accountant D. Financial controller

5. Which of the following will not be included in adjusted cash book?
A. Standing order B. Credit transfer C. Bank charges D. Un-credited checks

6. Bank charge of $12,000 was not entered in the cash book. Identify the correct adjustment in the cash book.
A. Debit cash book B. Add to cash book C. credit cash book D. Non-adjustment

7. Unpresented checks can also mean
A. A cancelled checks B. Dishonored checks C. Outstanding checks D. Uncollected checks

8. A checks returned by a bank marked "NSF" means that

A. Checks has been forged
B. Bank can't verify identity
C. There are no sufficient funds in the accounts
D. There are sufficient funds in the accounts

9. ----- are checks issued by a business entity but not yet paid by the bank on which it was drawn.
A. Un-credited checks B. Uncollected checks C. outstanding checks D. Bounced checks

10. Checks that are presented to bank but not yet credited by the bank is called
A. Un-deposited checks B. Unpresented checks C. Un-credited checks D. Bounced checks

11. Standing order is an instruction given to...... by..... to pay a regular amount of money to a third party.
A. An instructor, a recipient
B. A bank, an account holder
C. An account holder, a bank
D. An accountant, a lawyer

12. A company entered into a hire purchase contract to pay a regular payment of $20,000 per month. Four payments were made through its bank account but no entry was seen in the cash book. Identify the correct adjustment in the cash book.

A. Credit $20,000 B. Debit $20,000 C. Debit $80,000
D. Credit $80,000

13. In bank reconciliation statement, the amount of outstanding checks are added to ...... cash book balance
A. Adjusted B. Unadjusted C. bank balance D. Understated

14. Balance as per adjusted cash book = $4,500, un-credited checks =$2,500, unpresented checks = $3,000, cash in transit= $1,000. Calculate balance as per bank statement
A. $8,000 B. $4,000 C. $6,000 D. $5,000

15. Which of the following is not a cause of difference between balance as per cash book and balance as per bank statement?
A. Standing order B. paid check C. Unpresented checks D. Dishonored checks

Use the following question to answer question 16 and 17

	$
Balance as per cash book	16,000 Cr
Unpresented check	28,800
Un-credited check	5,200

A check of $4,000 paid to a creditor has been entered in error, in the cash column. Bank commission of $1,600 has not been entered in the cash book. The debit side of the cash book (bank column) had been under cast by $10,000.

16. The adjusted cash book balance is
A. $17,000Dr. B. $11,600Cr. C. $11,600Dr. D. $16,000Cr.

17. The balance as per bank statement is
A. $12,000 B $12,000 overdraft. C. $18,200 overdraft. D. $16,000

18. Which of the following does not appear in a bank statement
A. Dishonored check B. Bank charges C. Dividend received D. Un-credited check

19. A bank statement shows a debit balance of $16,600. After the entry of an un-credited check of $32,000, the balance is
A. $15,400 B.$ 48,600 C.$ 15,400 overdraft D. $16,600 overdraft

20. After comparing the cash book of a business entity with the bank statement, which of the following items could require an entry in the cash book?
i) un-credited check   ii) Dishonored check iii) bank charges iv) standing order v) credit transfer vi) cash withdrawal
A. i only   B. ii, iii, iv and v only   C. i and ii only   D. i, ii and vi only

21. When preparing a bank reconciliation statement, which of the following is added to the balance as per bank statement?
A. Bank charges. B. Un-credited checks
C. returned check D. Unpresented check.

22. Where the adjusted cash book does not show a debit balance in a bank reconciliation statement; unpresented checks are
A. deducted from the adjusted cash book balance
B. added to the adjusted cash book balance
C. added to the adjusted petty cash book balance
D. added to the petty cash

23. Which of the following will NOT affect the agreement of the cash book balance with the bank statement?
A. Cash payment B. Bank charges C. Unpresented check D. Dishonored check

24. Where a proprietor transfers cash from bank accounts to the supplier of the business entity, the entries would be
A. Debit Bank Account and Credit Cash Account
B. Credit Bank Account and Debit cash Account
C. Debit supplier Account and Credit Bank Account
D. Credit Proprietor's Account and Debit Supplier Accounts

25. Which of the following is a contra entry?
A. funds transferred to a supplier B. cash withdrawn for private use C. cash withdrawn from bank for office use. D. credit transfer

26. Which of the following is not important in the preparation of bank reconciliation statement?
A. Check counterfoil B. Cash book C. Bank statement D. Sales day book

Use the following information to answer questions 27 to 29.

CASH BOOK

		$			$
Jan.1	Bala	5,000	Jan. 1	Bal. b/d	12,500

Jan. 20	John	3,200	Jan. 10	Sade	2,400
Jan.29	Jane	2,240	Jan. 31	Musa	630
Jan. 31	Asa	2,060			
Jan. 31	Balance c/d	3,030			
		15,530			15,530

BANK STATEMENT

		DR	CR	Balance
		$	$	$
Jan. 1	Balance b/d			12,500 o/d
Jan. 1	Bala		5,000	7,500 o/d
Jan. 10	Sade	2,400		9,900 o/d
Jan. 20	John		3,200	6,700 o/d
Jan. 29	Jane		2,240	4,460 o/d
Jan. 30	Standing order	980		5,440 o/d
Jan. 31	Bank Charges	530		5,970 o/d

27. What is the total value of un-credited check?
   A. $1, 260 B. $2,240 C. $2,060 D. $1,500

28. What is the total value of unpresented check?
   A. $720 B. $630 C. $1,900 D. $2,400

29. What is the value of adjusted cash book balance?
A. $3,030   B. $5,970 O/D   C. $12,500 O/D   D. $4,540 O/D

Use the following information to answer question 30 – 31.

	$
Balance as per cash book	16,000
Unpresented check	28,800
Un-credited check	5,200

A check for $4,000 paid to a creditor has been entered in error, in the cash column. Bank commission of $1,600 had not been entered in the cash book. The debit side of the cash book (bank column) had been under cast by $10,000

30. The adjusted cash book balance is
  A. $20,400 CR B. $11,600 CR C. $20,400 DR D. $10,400CR

31. The balance as per bank statement is
A. $12,000 B. $11,600CR C. $28,800 D. $44,000

32. Which of the following might not be useful for preparing a bank reconciliation statement?
A. Bank Teller B. Bank Statement C. Cash Register D. Cash Book

33. Which of the following is NOT a reason why there could be differences between bank statements and cash book balances?
    i. Bank charges ii. Standing order iii. Presented checks
iv.Timing differences v. Credit Transfers vi. Bank lodgments.
A. ii only B. i and ii only C. iii and iv only D. iii and vi only

34. The Cash Book balance of a sole trader stood at $360,000. It was discovered that checks issued for $72,000 was entered in error as receipt. Bank charge of $74,000 was omitted. What is the adjusted cash book balance?
A. $142,000 B.$173,000 C. $ 214,000 D. $144,000

35. Cash deposited to bank appears as ....balance in the bank statement
A. debit B. credit C. prepayment D. liability

36. Cash withdrawn from bank by a proprietor of a business for personal use is recorded as.........balance in the bank statement
A. debit B. credit C. expenses D. income

37. Which of the following is not a document used to control bank accounts?
A. Bank statement B. pre-numbered checks C. electronic fund transfer slip D. pre-numbered card

38. Which of the following is not a necessary document for the preparation of bank reconciliation statement?
A. checks stub   B. Two column cash book   C. bank statement   D. petty cash book

39. A business had a balance at the bank of $5,200 at the start of the month. During the following month, it paid for goods invoiced at $2,000 less trade discount of 20%, and cash discount of 10%. It received a check from a customer in respect of an invoice for $500, subject to cash discount of 5%.
   What was the balance at the bank at the end of the month?
   A. $3,370 B. $3,380 C. $4,510 D. $4,235

40. Your firm's cash book at 31st December 2009 shows a balance at the bank of $3,250. Comparison with the bank statement at the same date reveals the following differences:
Unpresented checks $980, Bank charges not in cash book $64, Receipts not yet credited by the bank $590, Dishonored check not in cash book $295
What is the adjusted bank balance as per the cash book at 31st December 2009?
A. $2,891 B. $3,250 C. $359 D. $4,042

CHAPTER 6

DEPRECIATION AND NON-CURRENT ASSETS

1.   Depreciation is a/an
   A.   Physical wear and tear in the value of a tangible non-current asset as a result of usage
   B.   Reduction in the value of fixed asset
   C.   Destruction of a fixed asset
   D.   Impairment of asset as a result of usage

2.   Depreciation is charged on ......
   A.   Current asset B. Tangible Non- current asset C. Fixed debt   D. Goodwill

3.   Total depreciation plus residual value of a tangible non-current asset is the
   A.   Total expenditure   B. Accumulated depreciation   C. Cost of asset
   D.   Cost of fixed asset

4.   Book value of a tangible non- current asset is........
   A.   Market value
   B.   Cost of tangible non-current asset – accumulated depreciation
   C.   Historical cost of a fixed asset
   D.   Recoverable value of a tangible non- current asset

5.   The cost price of accounting packages that will be used for more than 12 months should be classified as........
   A.   Revenue expenditure B. Current asset C. Capital expenditure D. Historical cost

6.   In the calculation of depreciation, which of the following is not an estimate?
   A.   Salvage value B. Useful life C. Residual value D. Historical Value

7.   Which of the following is not an asset associated with depreciation?
    A. Land & Building B. Plant & Machinery C. Motor Vehicle D. Preliminary expenses

8.   HPY LTD. imported machinery from abroad, which of the following will not be included in the historical cost of the machinery that will appear in the balance sheet?
    A. Demurrage charges B. Purchase price of the machinery C. Signage duty D. Import Duty

9.   Where there is no additional assets or disposal of assets, provision for depreciation under straight line method
    A. Increases every year B. Reduces every year C. remains unchanged every year
    D. fluctuates

10.   The method of depreciation that allocates larger amount in the earlier years is called
    A. Straight line method B. Diminishing balance method C. Book value D. Residual value

    Use the following information to answer questions 11 to 14
    A machine cost $24,000 and has a useful life of 8 years, and expected disposal value of $800.

11.   Using the straight line method, what is the annual depreciation?
    A. $7,000 B. $9,002 C. $2,900 D. $3,000

12.   The accumulated depreciation at the end of year 6, using straight line method is
    A. $4,750 B. $17,400 C. $18,000 D. $14,500

13.   Using diminishing balance method, what will be the depreciation charge for year 2 at 25%? (ignoring residual value)
    A. $5,000 B. $4,500 C. $4,600 D. $13,500

14.   Using the reducing balance method, what is the net book value at the end of year 2? (ignore residual value)
    A. $14,500 B. $13,500 C. $4,500 D. $5,000

15.   A machinery costing $100,000 was depreciated at 20 per cent per annum by reducing balance method. Two years later, it was disposed for $60,000. The profit/loss was
    A. $6,000 profit B. $4,000 loss C. $4,000 profit D. $6,000 loss

16.   A business entity acquired a motor vehicle at $1,500,000. It is to be depreciated at a 20% per annum using the reducing balance method. What is the book value after year 2?
    A. $690,000 B. $960,000 C. $240,000 D.$ 300,000

17.   In the trial balance, the provision for depreciation account is
    A. Shown as a debit item
    B. Shown as a part of non- current asset
    C. Shown as a credit item
    D. Not shown

18. At the date of the statement of financial position, the balance on the accumulated provision for depreciation accounts is
    A. Transferred to profit and loss
    B. Transferred to the Depreciation Accounts
    C. Transferred to the asset Accounts
    D. Deducted from the asset in the statement of financial position.

19. Where an accumulated depreciation account is in use, then the entries for yearly depreciation is to
   A. Credit profit and loss account and debit depreciation accounts
   B. Credit asset account and debit provision for depreciation accounts
   C. Credit accumulated provision for depreciation accounts, debit profit and loss accounts
   D. Credit profit and loss account, debit asset accounts

20. A machine bought for $17,000 was estimated to have a useful life of 4years and a depreciation of $4,000 per annum. What is the scrap value of the asset?

   A. $2,000 B. $1,000   C. $1,500   D.$ 3,500

Use the following information to answer questions 21 to 23.
Equipment costing $120,000 was bought on 1st January 2001. Depreciation was provided at 20% annually on straight line method. It was sold on 30th June, 2004 for $31,500.

21. Its accumulated depreciation at the time of sales was
   A. $48,000 B. $84,000 C. $24,000 D. $48,000

22. In the year of sales, profit was......
   A. reduced by $4,500 B. reduced by $5,400 C. increased by $4,500 D. $5,400

23. The net book value of the asset at the time of sale was
   A. $63,000 B. $66,000 C. $36,000 D. $72,000

Use the following information to answer question 24 to 26.

The table below shows information concerning machinery imported from abroad.

	$
Purchase price of machinery	120,000
Import duty	11,000
Installation cost	5,500
Annual maintenance cost	1,400
Estimated useful life 5years	
Estimated scrap value	6,000

24. What is the total acquisition cost of the equipment?
    A. $125,500 B. $136,500 C.$ 120, 000 D. $137,900

25. Using reducing balance method, what is the depreciation charged for the second year (ignoring scrap value)?
    A. $27,300 B. $21,840 C. $26,500 D.$ 87,600

26. What is the annual depreciation charged if straight line method is used?
    A. $27,300 B. $26,100 C. $24,000 D.$ 25,100

27. Provision for the consumption of an asset of wasting character is called
    A. Provision for depreciation B. Provision for depletion C. Amortization D. impairment

28. Which of the following is not an asset of wasting characters?
    A. quarries B. oil wells C. mines D. equipment

29. Which of the following is not associated with amortization of assets?
    A. Patent right B. Copy right C. Machinery D. Goodwill

30. Which of the following is not a non- current asset?
    A. Goodwill B. inventory C. copy right D. oil wells

Use the following questions to answer questions 31 to 33

The purchase price of equipment is $10,000. Freight and installation costs are $1,500 and $1,800 respectively. The asset was depreciated at 20% per annum by the diminishing balance method. Two years later, it was sold for $5,000.

31. What is the historical cost of the equipment?
    A. $10,000 B. $13,300 C.$ 11,500 D.$ 11,800

32. The net profit or loss on the sale was
    A. $3,512 loss B. $1,712 loss C. $3,512 profit D. $212 loss

33. The net book value at the time of sale is
    A. $10,640 B. $8,512 C. $4,788 D. $2,128

34. The process of allocating the cost of an intangible asset over its useful life is known as
    A. Depreciation B. Depletion C. Amortization D. impairment

35. The depreciation for a machine was $18,400 in its 7th year of use. The depreciation for the asset in the 8th year of use was $19,750. What is the logical conclusion for this statement.
    A. There was an increase in the residual value of the machine
    B. There was a decrease in the residual value of the machine
    C. An additional machine was purchased
    D. Maintenance cost of the machine increased

Use the following information to answer question 36 and 37

Ambiba Enterprise had a non-current asset of $1,500,000 at the end of the year. Non-current assets costing $600,000 with provision for depreciation of $110,000 were disposed of during the period. Non-current assets of $92,000 were added during the year. Provision for depreciation was $250,000 at the beginning of the year, and $200,000 at the end of the year.

36. What was the cost of non-current assets at the beginning of the year?
     A. $2,800,000 B. $2,008,000 C. $2,100,000 D. $900,000

37. The depreciation expense charged for the year is
     A. $50,000 B. $150,000 C. $60,000 D. $100,000

38. The term used in describing a decrease in the quantity of available deposits of a wasting asset, as they are being extracted is............. reduction A. a demotion B. an amortization C. a depreciation D. a depletion

39. Which of the following does not belong to the group?
    A. Reducing balance B. Sum of the year's digits C. Accumulated depreciation D. Straight line

40. Which of the following may cause depreciation?
  i. obsolescence and passage of time
  ii. wear and tear
  iii. reduction in market value
     A. iii only B. iii only C. i and ii only D. I only

41. Where there is a provision for depreciation account, fixed assets should be shown in the balance sheet at..........
    A. Written down value B. historical value C. cost of acquisition
    D. historical cost less accumulated depreciation

42. Which of the following fixed assets is not depreciable
    A. Machinery B. Motor Vehicle C. Office building D. Land

Use the following question to answer question 43 to 45
A machine cost $420,000 and has a useful life of n years and an expected disposal value of $15,000 with annual depreciation of $84,000.

43. Using the straight-line method of depreciation, what is the useful life span of the machine to the nearest number of years?
    A. 4 years.
    B. 6 years.
    C. 7years.

D. 5 years.

44. Using the reducing balance method, what will be the depreciation charged for Year 2 (ignore residual value)?
    A. $80,000
    B. $67,200.
    C. $63,000
    D. $63,200.

45. Using the reducing balance method, what will be the net book value of the asset at the end of year 3?
    A. $430,400.
    B. $198,000.
    C. $215,040.
    D. $261,200.

CHAPTER 7

CONTROL ACCOUNTS

1. One of the following is a major purpose for preparing control accounts
   A. Computation of income
   B. Correction of errors in the accounts
   C. Detection of errors in the accounts
   D. Transferring entries to other accounts

2. Sales ledger control account can also be called
   A. Statement of Cash flow
   B. Total Accounts receivable Account
   C. Total Accounts payable Account
   D. Sales day book

3. Bad debt written off during an account period is recorded on which side of the control accounts
   A. Debit side of total accounts receivable account
   B. Credit side of total accounts payable account
   C. Debit side of total accounts payable account
   D. Credit side of total accounts receivable account

4. Purchases ledger control accounts shows the following:
   Purchases = $800, discount received = $120, bank = $450, balance c/d = $500
   What is the balance b/d?
   A. $270 B. $170 C. $200 D. $30

5. Which of the following statement is/are correct?
   1. Total Debtors account is total accounts receivable account
   2. Total Debtors account is Sales Ledger Control accounts
   3. Total Debtors account is Sales accounts
   4. Total creditors account is total accounts payable account

5. Total creditors account is purchases ledger control account
A. 1, 2, 4 and 5 only   B.1, 2 and 3 only   C. 2 and 3 only   D. Non of the above

6. Which of the following does not appear in a sales ledger control accounts?
A. Bank and cash   B. Discount allowed   C. Dishonored check   D. Provision for doubtful debts

7. Which of the following is the balance in the purchases ledger control accounts?
A. total sales   B. total purchases   C. total debtors   D. total creditors

8. Micki who has two accounts with Jev. Ltd agreed to have only one outstanding balance. By which of the following methods could this be done?
A. Suspense account entry   B. Contra entry   C. Adjustment entry   D. Double entry

9. A contra entry of $500 between sales ledger and purchases ledger was omitted from sales ledger control account. Which of the following is the correct adjustment in accounts payable control account?
A. $500 should be debited
B. $1,000 should be debited
C. $500 should be credited
D. No adjustment is required

You are required to answer question 10 to 13 from the following information.

Sales Ledger Control Accounts

	$		$
Balance b/d	?	Discount Allowed	768
Sales	21,410	Returns inwards	742
Check dishonored	342	Cash received from customers	?

	Balance c/d	13,540
34,542		34,542

10. What is the total debt at the end of the year?
    A. $21,410 B. $13,540 C. $34,542 D. $15,013

11. What is the net sales for the year?
    A. $21,410 B. $20,668 C. $34,542 D. $742

12. What is the total cash received from customers?
    A. $19,492 B. $13,540 C. $768 D. $21,410

13. What is the total debt at the beginning of the year?
    A. $12,790 B. $21,410 C. $14,500 D. $13,540

14. One of the advantages of Control Accounts is that
    A. all errors are generalized
    B. all errors are located
    C. all errors are pending
    D. all errors are deducted

15. Which of the following is not an item of total accounts receivable account?
    A. Dishonored check B. Cash received from customers C. Cash sales
    E. Bills receivable

16. In the absence of a sales day book or sales account, the credit for sales can be computed from

    A. total accounts payable account
    B. total accounts receivable account
    C. opening figures of the balance sheet
    D. closing figures of the balance sheet

17. From which of the following sources are total accounts payable account most likely to be posted?
    A. Customer's invoices

B. Cash disbursements journal
C. Supplier's invoices
D. Purchases journal

18. Creditors at the beginning was $609,000 and closing creditors balance was $96,000, check issued to suppliers during the year amounting $906,000. What is the credit purchases for the year?
   A. $1,002,000 B. $393,000 C. $960,000 D. $906,000

19. Which of the following items will be found on the credit side of Sales Ledger Control Accounts.
   A. Debtors' check dishonored B. Credit sales C. Bad debts written-off
   D. Interest on overdue account

Use the following information to answer question 20 and 21.

	1st Jan.	31st Dec.
	$	$
Payables	6,000	10,500
Inventory	4,000	6,400

Cash paid to suppliers during the year was $37,000

20. Purchases for the year was
   A. $18,000 B. $91,000 C. $41,500 D. $40,000

21. What was the cost of sales for the year?
   A. $93,100 B. $16,000 C. $13,000 D. $39,100

22. Which of the following is not a credit item in the purchases ledger control accounts?
   A. Bills payable B. discount received C. credit purchases D. Interest on overdue debt

23. Which of the following is not a credit item in the sales ledger control accounts?
   A. Returned inward B. Discount allowed C. Cash paid D. Dishonored check

Use the following information to answer question 23 – 25

	$
Opening Inventory	2,000
Closing Inventory	1,600
Accounts Payable - 1/1/2008	1,500
Accounts Payable - 31/12/2008	1,280
Cash paid to suppliers	7,200
Accounts Receivable - 1/1/2008	580
Cash received from customers	12,240
Accounts Receivable - 31/12/2008	420

24. Sales for the year was
A. $16,000 B.$ 6,980 C.$ 12,080 D. $7,380

25. Cost of sales for the year was
A. $16,090 B.$ 12,080 C.$ 5,990 D. $7,380

26. Gross profit for the year was
A.$ 4,300 B. $3,500 C. $4,700 D. $7,380

27. A technique used for finding missing figure in incomplete records is
   A. journal proper   B. ledger   C. control accounts   D. sales journal

Use the following information to answer question 28 and 29

	$
Opening receivables	60,000
Opening payables	50,000
Credit sales	105,000
Credit purchases	95,000
Bad debts written off	6,500
Set-offs	77,000

28. Closing receivable is
   A. $81,500 B. $19,800 C. $77,000 D. $68,000

29. What is the closing balance of accounts payables?

A. $41,600 B. $68,000 C. $81,500 D. $77,000

30. Which of the following is a self-balancing account?
A. Appropriation Account B. Suspense Account C. Control Account D. Assets Account

31. Discount allowed to customer for earlier settlement of bill will be
   A. Credited purchases ledger control accounts
   B. Debited purchases ledger control account
   C. Credited to Sales ledger control accounts
   D. Debited to Sales ledger control accounts

32. In a sales ledger control account, contra entry is found on the
   A. debit side of the sales ledger control account
   B. debit side of the purchases ledger control account
   C. credit side of the sales ledger control account
   D. credit side of the purchases ledger control account

Use the following information to answer question 33 and 34.

Opening accounts payable balance = $21,280, purchases= $53,824, return inward= $1,969, return outward = $1,620, cash discount received = $2,696, cash discount allowed = $2,500
Cash paid to suppliers = $41,616.
At the year-end, the purchases ledger showed a debit balance of $216.

33. The outstanding balance in the purchases ledger control account is
    A. $29,388 B.$ 16,500 C. $29,604 D. $75,320

34. The total debit balance on the purchases ledger control accounts is
    A. $75,320 B. $29,604 C.$ 216 D. $24,019

Use the following information to answer question 35 to 37.

	$		$
Balance b/d	17,200	Balance b/d	2,204
Total sales	106,620	Total bank receipts	90,070
Dishonored check	4,400	Total discounts	3,930
Balance c/d	2,288	Total returns	2,720
		Purchases ledger	4,040
		Balance c/d	27,544
	130,508		130,508

35. What is the title of the ledger account shown above?
A. Sales Ledger
B. Purchases Ledger
C. Sales Ledger Control Accounts
D. Purchases Ledger Control Accounts

36. The balance of $27,544 represents
A. Outstanding balance due to suppliers
B. Outstanding balance due from customers
C. Outstanding balance due to customers
D. Balancing figure

37. The entry purchases ledger $4,040 means
A. Trade debtor's balances set-off against debt on purchases
B. Cash purchases
C. Credit purchases
D. Cash sales

38. Opening Total Creditors $325,000; Closing Total Creditors $205,000; Credit purchases $1,000,000; discount received $15,000; discount allowed $32,000 and sales ledger contra $175,000. How much was paid to the creditors according to the available information?
A. $309,000 B. $930,000 C. $1,280,000 D. $125,000

39. Total purchases is taken from which book of accounts for the preparation of purchases ledger control accounts?
A. Petty cash book   B. Sales journal C. Purchases journal D. invoice

40. What are the correct entries for return inward and return outward respectively in control accounts?
   A. Debit purchases ledger control account and credit sales ledger control accounts
   B. Credit purchases ledger control accounts and debit sales ledger control accounts
   C. Debit sales ledger control accounts and debit purchases ledger control accounts
   D. Credit sales ledger control accounts and debit purchases ledger control accounts

CHAPTER 8

ACCOUNTING FOR NON- PROFIT ORIENTED ORGANIZATIONS

1. In a not-for-profit organization, the excess of income over expenditure is
   - A. added to cash balance.
   - B. added to capital
   - C. deducted from accumulated fund.
   - D. added to accumulated fund.

2. The equivalent of club's statement of comprehensive income is
   - A. Revenue Accounts
   - B. Profit and Loss Accounts
   - C. Income and Expenditure Accounts
   - D. Receipts and Payment Accounts

3. The difference between assets and liabilities of a club or society is
   - A. Capital B. Equity C. Accumulated fund D. Working capital

4. Subscription in advance is treated in the balance sheet of a club as
   - A. Current asset B. Current liability C. Reserve D. Fictitious asset

5. Which of the following is a credit item on an income and expenditure accounts?
   - A. Salaries B. Bar expenses C. Subscription D. Rates

6. The equivalent of a club's Receipt and Payment accounts is a
   - A. Trading account B. Cash Book C. Profit and Loss Account
   - D. Revenue accounts

7. A non-profit-making organization differs from a profit making on in that
   - A. it does not earn income
   - B. proceeds from sale of shares form part of its income
   - C. all its income is committed
   - D. annual subscriptions and levies form part of its income

8. Subscription in advance is an example of ....in the book of a club.

  A. accrual B. deposit C. prepayment D. receivables

9. Income and expenditure accounts is based on
  A. Accrual Accounting
  B. Cash accounting
  C. Financial Accounting
  D. Management Accounting

10. The debit balance on the receipt and payment account of a non-profit organization is regarded as a
  A. Current liability
  B. Current Asset
  C. Accrual
  D. Prepayment

11. Which of the following is the accounting equation for non-profit organization?
  A. Asset = Capital + Liability
  B. Asset = Liability + Fund
  C. Accumulated fund + Liability = Asset
  D. Capital = Asset – liability

12. A non-profit organization received $6,000 as the entrance fee of a new member. If 15% of the fee has to be capitalized, what is the amount of fee needed to be shown in the income and expenditure account?
  A. $6,100 B. $900 C.$ 5,100 D.$ 7,500

13. The end result of Income and expenditure accounts of a club shows
  A. Net Profit or Net Loss B. Gross Profit C. Surplus or deficit
  E. Cash available to the club

Use the following information to answer question 14 and 15
  $25,000 received as the annual membership subscription. Out of this, $3,000 is meant for previous accounting period whereas $1,500 is receivable at the end of the current accounting period.

14. Calculate the amount of subscription that will be shown in the income and expenditure account for the current accounting period.
   A. $22,500 B.$ 23,500 C. $26,500 D. $6,500

15. How much will be recorded as a current asset in the balance sheet?
   A. $1,500 B.$ 2,500 C.$ 3,000 D.$ 25,000

16. When cash is received for life membership, which of the following double entries is recorded?
   A. Debit life membership account and credit income and expenditure account
   B. Debit life membership accounts and credit cash accounts
   C. Debit cash accounts and credit life membership accounts
   D. Debit life membership accounts and credit investment

17. Depreciation of an asset is matched against the revenue of a not-for profit organization in its
A. cash book   B. profit and loss account   C. income and expenditure account   D. accumulated depreciation

Use the following information to answer question 18 to 20

The following information relates to a Tennis club:

	$
Subscription owing at the beginning	80
Subscription owing at the end	65
Subscription received in advance at the Beginning	25
Subscription received during the accounting period	2,560

18. The amount to be shown in the income and expenditure account would be
A. $2,500 B. $2,570   C. $2,300 D. $2,590.

19. The amount to be recorded as current liability is
A. $3,300   B. $0   C. $2,400   D.$ 65

20. How much will be recorded as a current asset in the balance sheet as at the end of the accounting period?
A. $25   B.$ 65   C. $80   D. $250

21. Which of the following is not an item of receipt and payment accounts?
A. Donation   B. Depreciation   C. honorarium   D. subscription

Use the following information to answer question 22 to 23.

The following were extracted from the book of J.V club as at 31st December, 2014:

	$
Furniture	500,000
Sport kit	800,000
Club house	750,000
Subscription prepaid	20,000
Bar Creditors	312,000
Subscription owing	90,000

22. Compute the accumulated fund as the period
A. $1,900,000   B. $1,808,000   C. $800,000   D. $750,000

23. Compute the total current asset as at the period.
A. $750,000   B. $ 190,000   C. $20,000   D. $90,000

Use the following questions to answer question 24 to 27
The following are extracted from the books of Vilili Rotary Club.

Receipt and payment as the year ended 31st December, 2009.

	$		$
Balance b/d	2,000	Salaries	4,000
Subscription	30,000	Rent	2,000
		Rates	3,000
		Electricity expenses	1,000

	Balance c/d	22,000
32,000		32,000
Balance b/d 22,000		

	1st January, 2009	31st December, 2009
	$	$
Equipment	120,000	120,000
Rent(accrued)	400	500
Rates(prepaid)	600	800
Subscription in arrears	3,000	2,000
Subscription in advance	2,600	1600

24. What is the accumulated fund as at 1st January, 2009?
A. $131,000   B. $126,000   C. $125,600   D. $122,600

25. Subscription relating to the year 2009 is
A. $30,000   B.$ 56,000   C.$ 31,200   D.$ 18,000

26. What is the amount of subscription that will appear on the credit side of income and expenditure account for the year 2009?
A. $31,200   B.$18,000   C. $56,000   D. $30,000

27. Rates charged to the income and expenditure account for the year 2009 is
A. $3,900   B.$2,000   C. $2,800   D. $4,600

Use the following information to answer questions 28 and 29.

Income and Expenditure Account

	$		$
Wages	28,000	Subscription received	60,000
Electricity	10,000	Donations	30,000
Depreciation of furniture	3,000	Profit on sales of cars	5,000
Other expenses	?		
Excess of	?		

income over expenditure		
95,000		95,000

It is the tradition of the club to write off an amount equal to 30% of the subscription received as other expenses.

28. What is the amount to be written off other expenses?
A. $25,000   B. $18,000   C.$ 17,000   D. $60,000

29. What is the amount of the surplus?
A. $37,000   B.$36,000   C.$ 18,000   D. $63,000

30. Net profit is for Profit and Loss Account, while Surplus is for
A. Receipt and Payments Account
B. Receipts and Expenditure Account
C. Income and Expenditure Account
D. Revenue and payment Account

31. Subscription received but not yet earned is recorded under
A. assets   B. current liabilities   C. equity   D. non- current assets

32. Which of the following will not be found in the statement of financial position of a non-profit-oriented organization?
A. assets   B. liabilities   C. accumulated funds   D. owners' equity

33. Investment in sinking fund by a non-profit-oriented organization is know as
A. assets   B. liabilities   C. bonds   D. expenditures

34. Which of the following are sources of income for non-trading organization?
    i. donation   ii. government subvention   iii. subscription   iv. Proceeds from social activities   v. proceed from disposal of asset   vi. government bond
    A. i,ii,iii and iv only   B. ii and vi only
    C. i, ii, iii, iv and v only   D. i, ii, iii, iv, v and vi only

35. A statement of affairs as at the start of an accounting period is drawn up to determine which of the following?

A. Share of profit due to members B. subscription owed
C. capital   D. accumulated fund

36. In a non-profit-oriented organization, depreciation of asset is recorded to which account?
    A. profit and loss accounts
    B. receipt and payment accounts
    C. trading accounts
    D. income and expenditure accounts

37. On what basis are the receipt and payment accounts prepared?
    A. accrual basis   B. commitment basis   C. cash basis D. income basis

38. The main purpose of preparing income and expenditure accounts is to determine
A. Net profit or loss for the period
B. Gross profit or loss for the period
C. Accumulated fund for the period
D. Surplus or deficit for the period

39. Which of the following is the accounting basis for recording donation received by a non-profit-oriented organization?
A. cash basis B. accrual basis C. materiality D. commitment basis

40. An amount paid as honorarium by non-profit-oriented organization is
A. debited to statement of comprehensive income
B. credited to income and expenditure accounts
C. debited to income and expenditure accounts
D. transferred to members of the organization

CHAPTER 9

MANUFACTURING ACCOUNTS

1. Prime costs consist of
   A. Overhead cost
   B. Direct cost and overhead cost
   C. Direct expenses and direct labor
   D. Direct expenses, direct material and direct labor

   Use the following information to answer questions 5 to 7

	$
Manufacturing cost of finished goods	182,000
Selling and distribution	16,000
Salary	28,000
Mark-up is 15%	

2. The gross profit for the year is
   A. $ 27,300 B. $24,000 C. $28,000 D. $30,000

3. The net profit or net loss is
   A. Net profit of $16,700 B. Net profit of $18,000 C. Net loss of $2,400 D. Net loss of $16,700

4. In a manufacturing organization, which of the following expenses will not be included in the cost of production
   A. Direct labor cost B. Direct overhead C. direct material cost
   D. Administrative overhead

5. A business entity which process raw material to become finished goods
   Prepares
   A. Statement of comprehensive income and statement of financial position

B. Manufacturing accounts, Trading, Profit and Loss Account and Balance sheet
C. Trading, profit and loss accounts and balance sheet
D. Balance sheet only

6. Wages paid to an operator in a manufacturing company increases ----
   A. Factory cost B. Overhead C. Prime cost D. Gross profit

7. Which of the following will not be included in a cost of production?
   A. cost of material consumed B. Work-in-progress C. carriage outward D. direct labor

Use the following information to answer question 8 to 12
The following transaction was extracted from the book of Jeje Ltd as
at 31st, Dec. 2010.

	$
Opening stock of raw materials	16,000
Closing stock of raw materials	14,700
Raw material purchased	29,000
Carriage outwards	2,300
Direct labor	8,000
Electricity	7,500
Supervisor salary	10,000
Depreciation of plant	3,000
Sales `	110,000
Closing stocks (finished Goods)	4,500
Administrative expenses	10,500

Note: 2/3 of electricity was used in the factory while 1/3 of electricity was used in office

8. The cost of raw material consumed is
   A. $30,300 B.$47,300 C. $32,600 D. $45,000

9. The prime cost is

A. $40,600 B. $38,300 C. $30,300 D. $18,000

10. What is the value of factory overhead?
A. $20,000 B. $18,000 C. $38,900 D. $81,000

11. What is the total cost of production?
A. $56,300 B. $18,000 C. $58,600 D. $38,300

12. Calculate the gross profit.
A. $56,200 B. $58,200 C. $55,900 D. $45,400

13. The cost of raw material consumed is determined in the manufacturing
    account as
    A. Cost of material available plus opening stock
    B. Cost of material available plus closing stock
    C. Cost of raw material available less closing raw material
    D. Opening stock plus purchases less closing stock

14. The addition of Prime cost and Factory Overheads is
    A. Cost of sales B. Cost of goods consumed
    C. Cost of production D. Market Value

15. The difference between factory cost of goods produced
and its market value is
    A. Gross profit B. Manufacturing profit C. Net profit D. interest

16. The factory cost of goods produced is made up of
    A. Raw material consumed and factory overhead
    B. Factory cost and work-in progress
    C. Prime cost and factory overhead
    D. Raw material available and market price

Given that:

	$
Prime cost	137,500
Indirect manufacturing cost	66,400
Work in progress at start	4,500

Work in progress at close   5,200

17. Determine the production cost
A. $305,600   B.$ 203,200   C. $208,400   D.$ 203,900

18. The gross profit on manufactured goods is the difference between the cost of goods manufactured and the
A. Market value of goods produced
B. Prime cost of production
C. Indirect cost of production
D. Finished goods produced.

Use the following information to answer questions 19 to 23.

	$
Raw material:	
Stock1 /1/2004	9,000
Purchases	58,000
Stock 31/12/2004	11,000
Direct wages	68,000
Indirect wages	21,600
Factory expenses:	
Rent	36,000
Insurance	6,000
Royalties	1,000
Carriage inward	2,400
Work-in-progress 1/1/2004	7,500
Work-in-progress 31/12/2004	13,500

19. What is the cost of raw-material available for production?
A. $67,000 B. $69,400 C.$ 58,400 D.$ 76,000

20. What is the cost of raw material consumed?
A. $69,400 B.$ 70,000 C. $58,400 D. $67,000

21. The prime cost is
A. $127,400 B. $69,000 C. $21,600 D. $76,000

22.The amount of factory overhead
A. $36,600 B. $63,600 C. $127,400 D. $191,000

23. The cost of goods manufactured is
A. $185,000 B. $198,500 C. $191,000 D. $154,000

24. In a manufacturing concern, which of the following is a component of prime cost?
A. Factory expenses
B. carriage outward
C. Royalty
D. Sales commission

25. Spare parts of machinery are examples of
A Indirect materials B. Direct material
C. Indirect expenses D. Direct expenses

26. Which of the following is a direct cost to a manufacturing company?
A. Factory supervisor's salary
B. Machine operator's wages
C. Salesman's commission
D. Wages of factory cleaners

27. The following were extracted from the books of J.J. books.

31st December, 2009:

| Raw material | $200,000 |

31st December, 2009:

| Work-in-progress | $85,000 |

31st December, 2008:

| Finished goods | $120,000 |

31st December, 2009:

| Finished goods | $68,000 |

31st December, 2008:

Work-in-progress $86,000

What is the total inventory that will appear in its statement of financial position as at 31st December, 2009?
   A. $353,000 B. $533,000 C. $371,000 D. $200,000

28. If the following are the only information available:
  Total production cost is $520,000 and the total overhead cost is $210,000. What is the prime cost?
   A. $310,000 B. $520,000 C. $730,000 D. $160,000

29. Given that the prime cost is $116,000, indirect manufacturing cost is $68,000 and closing work in progress is $38,000. What is the total manufacturing cost?
   A. $184,000 B. $222,000 C. $86,000 D. $146,000

30. The following are the inventories of a manufacturing company Except
   A. work-in-progress B. raw material C. finished goods D. spare parts

CHAPTER 10

PARTNERSHIP ACCOUNTS

1. Which of the following is NOT a basis of sharing partnership profits?
A. Capital invested
B. Time spent on partnership business
C. Expertise or experience
D. Age of partners.

2. If $72,000 was debited to a partner's current account and the sales account credited with the same amount, this means that
   A. goods have been purchased from the partner.
   B. the partner has returned goods to the firm
   C. the partner withdrew goods from stock and was charged at cost price
   D. goods have been sold to the partner

3. Goodwill can be valued in partnership when,
   A. partners make profits
   B. losses are recorded
   C. a partner retires
   D. a new branch is opened

4. The written agreement of partnership is commonly called....
   A. Partnership Act   B. Partnership Deed   C. Partnership Contract
   D. Memo

5. Where no partnership agreement exist between partners, partners will share profit
   A. According to capital contributed by each partner
   B. According to the level of expertise
   C. According to the level of work undertaken
   D. Equally

6. Under the fluctuating capital method, what is the treatment for interest on capital?
   A. Credited to current accounts
   B. Credited to capital accounts
   C. Debited to current accounts
   D. Debited to capital accounts

7. Under Fixed capital method, what is the treatment for interest on capital?
   A. Credited to capital accounts
   B. Debited to capital accounts
   C. Credited to current account
   D. Debited to current accounts

8. .... is a value addition to a business because of reputation of business, and
      Customer's patronage and loyalty
      A. Business name B. Goodwill C. Market penetration D. Capital appreciation

9. Payment of salaries to partners is
      A) An appropriation of interest on capital
      B) A charge to profit and loss account
      C) A charge to trading account
      D) A charge to Profit and loss appropriation accounts

Use the following information to answer question 10 to 13
John and Audu are in partnership with the following partnership agreement:

	John	Audu
	$	$
Fixed Capital	30,000	50,000
Salary per annum	12,000	16,000
Interest on capital per annum	12%	12%
Profit or loss sharing ratio	40%	60%

The net profit for the year ended 31st December 1999 is $58,000 while drawings are
$5,000 and $7,000 for John and Audu respectively.

10. What is the total interest on capital?
   A. $6,300 B. $3,600 C. $6,000 D.$ 9,600

11. What is the profit available for distribution?
   A. $4,000 B. $12,400 C. $20,400 D.$ 30,000

12. What is John's share of the profit?
   A. $20,400 B. $12,240 C. $8,160 D. $12,000

13. What is the Audu's share of the profit?
   A. $12,240 B. $8,160 C. $12,000 D. $20,400

14. Goodwill is a/an
   A. current asset B. current liability C. intangible asset D. wasting asset

15. Partner's drawing is debited to partners'
   A. Interest Accounts B. Current Accounts C. personal Accounts
   D. Loan Accounts

Use the following information to answer questions 16 to 21.

Clem and Smith are in a partnership business, sharing profit and losses in the ratio
3:2 . Other information is as follows:

Capital:	
Clem	$40,000
Smith	$20,000
Drawings:	
Clem	$5,000
Smith	$7,000
Interest on capital	5%
Interest on drawings	10%
Net Profit	$14,000

16. What is the interest on smith's capital?
   A. $2,000 B. $1,000 C. $3,000 D.$ 700

17. Interest on Clem's drawings is

A. $500 B. $700 C. $2,000 D.$ 1,000

18. What is Clem share of profit?
   A. $3,920 B. $7,320 C. $4,080 D. $5,880

19. What is Smith's share of the profit
   A. $3,920 B. $5,880 C. $4,880 D. $6,120

20. What is the balance on Clem's Current Accounts?
   A. $2,620DR B. $3,820CR C.$ 3,120CR D.$ 1,920DR

21. What is the balance on Smith's Current Accounts
   A. $1,820 DR B. $3,820DR. C. $2,620 CR D. $3,120DR

22. Where there is no partnership agreement, any fund invested by a partner into the partnership in excess of agreed capital, attracts

   A. Interest at the rate of 10% per annum
   B. Interest at the rate of 2.5% per annum
   C. Interest at the rate of 15% per annum
   D. Interest at the rate of 5% per annum

23. Which of the following is not true of partnership business without written agreement?
   A. Profit and losses will be shared equally
   B. salaries are not allowed to partners
   C. Additional fund invested into partnership by any partner
      attracts 5% interest D. Interest of 5% is paid on drawings

24. The main differentiating element between the final accounts of a partnership and a sole trader is the
   A. drawings account B. appropriation account
   C. capital account   D. debtors accounts

Use the following information to answer question 25 to 27.

John and Paul are in partnership but there is no partnership agreement. The capital contributed is $90,000 by John and $60,000 by Paul. Profit for the year is $30,000.

25. What is Paul's share of the profit?
   A. $20,000   B. $15,000   C. $30,000   D. $10,000

26. What is John's share of the profit?
   A. $20,000   B. $10,000   C. $15,000   D. $30,000

27. If John introduced cash of $15,000 by way of loan to the partnership, how much interest will he earn per annum on the loan?
   A. $1, 500   B. $750   C. $500   D. $10,500

Use the following information to answer question 28 to 30

	J. Smith	P. Lucia
	$	$
Current Accounts balance (April 1,1990)	8,000	12,000
Current Accounts balance (April 1,1991)	14,000	?
Drawings	3,000	3,000
Shares of net profit	?	5,000

28. What is J. Smith's share of the profit from the partnership for the year ended March 31, 1991.
   A. $18,000   B. $9,000   C. $8,000   D. $5,000

29. What is P. Lucia's Current Accounts balance for the year ended March 31, 1991.
   A. $45,000   B. $14,000   C. $12,000   D. $5,000

30. Their profit sharing ratio is
   A. 3.6 : 2   B. 1.8 : 1   C. 2:2   D. 1:1

31. Partners whose liabilities are limited to the financial contribution to the partnership business in the event of liquidation are
   A. Sleeping partners   B. Dormant partners   C. Limited partners   D. Managing partners

Use the following information to answer question 32

Year	Profit
2010	$70,000

| 2011 | $92,000 |
| 2012 | $99,000 |

32. The value of goodwill purchased calculated at 3-year purchase of annual profit is
 A. $78,000 B. $99,000 C.$87,000 D. $88,000

33. Which of the following is not found in a partnership statement of financial position?
 A. Capital   B. Drawings C. Accounts receivable D. Accounts payable

34. An item of appropriation in partnership profit and loss account is.
A. interest on partners' capital
B. interest on partners' loan
C. employees' salaries
D. partners drawings

35. The partnership Deed ordinarily specifies
A. how profits or losses are to be shared
B. the capital to be contributed annually
C. how salaries are paid to employees
D. the profit that should be earned annually

36. Which of the following is correct concerning the cost of partnership dissolution?
   A. debit realization account and credit bank/cash account
   B. debit realization accounts and credit capital accounts
   C. credit capital account and debit bank account
   D. debit bank account and credit realization accounts

37. Which of the following is a method of Goodwill valuation?
  A. Average capital method
  B. Revaluation method
  C. Super capital method
  D. Super profit method

38. The main account in which dissolution of partnership entries are made is known as

A. dissolution accounts
B. revaluation accounts
C. Realization accounts
D. Disposal accounts

39. Partner "Y" took a firm's vehicle worth $112,000 without payment at the time of firm's dissolution.
    Identify the correct adjustment in the book of partner "Y".
    A. $112,000 will be debited to Y's appropriation account
    B. $112,000 will be credited to Y's capital account
    C. $112,000 will be debited to Y's capital account
    D. No entry is needed

40. During the process of dissolution of partnership, the carrying value of building $= \$100,000$ and motor vehicle $= \$50,000$ while both assets were disposed at the cumulative price of $140,000 and cost of dissolution was $3,000. Identify the total amount needed to be credited or debited to partners' capital accounts
    A. $119,000Dr B. $14,000Cr C. $13,000Dr D. $13,000 Cr

41. A partner that does not participate in the management of partnership business, but he or she has invested in the business and liable to creditors of the business is known as
    A. Active partner B. Limited partner C. Dormant partner D.
       Nominal partner

42. A and B are in partnership business. Their profit or loss sharing ratio is 3:2. A new Partner C is admitted in the business that will share profit or loss in the ratio 1/4. Which of the following is the new partnership profit sharing ratio?
    A. 18:15:10 B. 9: 5: 6 C. 3:2: 1 D. 9:6:5

43. Identify the correct double entry for realization profit during the time of dissolution of Partnership
    A. Debit partners' capital accounts and credit realization accounts
    B. Debit partners' capital accounts and credit dissolution accounts
    C. Credit realization accounts and debit partners' capital accounts
    D. Debit realization accounts and credit partners' capital accounts

44. Umar and Ahmed share profits and losses equally and have capital balances of $60,000 and $80,000 respectively. If Abdullahi purchases a 1/4ᵗʰ interest with no bonus, how much will he have to contribute to the partnership?
A. $44,000   B. $43,000
C. $35,000   D. $70,000

45. In which of the following circumstances is Goodwill Valued?
A. partners become old
B. large losses are made
C. a new partner is admitted
D. a new branch is opened

46. Which of the following is not a need for revaluation of Partnership Assets?
A. The partners change the profit and loss sharing ratio
B. A new partner is admitted
C. A partner leaves the firm
D. A partner becomes old.

47. Any loss on revaluation account should be
A. Credited to old partners' capital account in the old profit-sharing ratio
B. Debited to old partners' capital account in the old profit sharing ratio
C. Debited to new partners' capital account in the new profit sharing ratio
D. Credited to new partners' capital accounts in the new profit sharing ratio

48. Which of the following is an objective for revaluation of assets if partnership changes?
A. To obey the law
B. To prevent fraud
C. To prevent injustice to some partners
D. To make an adjustment for inflation

49. The accounting entry to record the premium on goodwill is to debit
A. bank and credit old partners' capital

B. goodwill and credit revaluation
C. assets and liability
D. capital and credit assets

50. When a new partner is admitted to a partnership there is a need to revalue the
A. capital of the business
B. capital and liabilities of the business
C. assets and capital of the business
D. assets and liabilities of the business

.

CHAPTER 11

COMPANY'S ACCOUNTS

1. Which of the following is not an amount stated in the Memorandum of Association as the amount of capital to be issued and upon which stamp duty has been paid?
   - A. registered capital
   - B. nominal capital
   - C. authorized capital
   - D. called-up capital

2. When shares are oversubscribed, the promoter may decide to scale down the number of shareholding. When this is done, the shares are being

   A. Issued at a discount   B. issued at par   C. issued at a premium
   D. issued at a high price

3. Authorized share capital of a limited liability company is the number of shares
   - A. Called up B. offered for sales C. subscribed D. approved in the memorandum of association

4. Preliminary expenditure of a limited liability company is a
   - A. Current liability B. current asset C. Non-current asset D. non current liability

5. AMAXI Company Limited issued common stock of $1 each to the public at $1.50. The shares were issued at
   - A. Par B. a discount C. a premium D. a profit

6. MPL Limited has authorized share capital of 200,000 $1 common stock of which 150,000 were issued at $1.20. All the issued shares are fully paid. Dividend declared is 5%. How much is the dividend shown in the Appropriation Account?
   - A. $9,000 B.$ 12,000 C.$ 7,500 D.$ 10,000

7. The excess of the par value of a company's shares over the amount for which they are issued to the public is called

A. par B. discount C. premium D. reserve

8. The maximum amount which a company can raise by way of selling shares is
   A. Share capital B. Authorized capital C. Issued capital D.paid-up capital

9. Part of the authorized share capital that has not been allotted to members is called
   A. Uncalled capital B. Unissued capital C. Unpaid capital D. paid capital

10. The undistributed profit of a limited liability company is called
   A. Accumulated fund B. Retained earnings C. Net profit D. Gross profit

11. Shares of a company can be classified into two main types
   A. Redeemable shares and irredeemable shares
   B. Preferred stock and common stock
   C. Issued shares and unissued shares
   D. Non of the above

12. Profit made prior to incorporation is credited to
   A. General reserve.
   B. Capital reserve.
   C. Revenue reserve.
   D. Profit and loss Account.

13. Capital reserve can be used in any of the following ways EXCEPT:
   A. Issuing bonus shares.
   B. Writing-off fictitious assets.
   C. Writing-off intangible assets.
   D. Distribution of dividend to stockholders.

14. The document setting out the regulations regarding meetings and internal organization of a company is known as
   A. memorandum of association B. articles of association
   C. prospectus D. company law.

Use the following question to answer question 15 to 16

A limited liability company has an authorized share capital of 100 million, $1 each split into 200 million shares. 160 million shares were offered for subscription at 60 cents per share payable in full on application. These have been fully subscribed and issued.

15. What is the nominal value of each share?
   A. $2   B. $0.80   C.$0.60   D. $0.50

16. What is the issued capital?
   A. $50million   B.$ 68million
   C. $50million   D.$ 80million.

17. Expenses incurred when incorporating a company are
   A. financial expenses   B. preliminary expenses   C. ordinary expenses   D.office expenses

18. The underwriter for a company's share is paid
   A. interest B. commission C. remuneration D. dividend

19. Which of the following is an element of memorandum of association?
   A. Name of directors B. Business objective C. appointment of directors   D. payment of dividend

20. A document which advertises the sales of shares of a company is known as
   A. Journal   B. Prospectus   C. Trust deed   D. Debenture certificate

21. Which of the following attracts a fixed rate of dividend?
   A. Debenture   B. common stock   C. Preferred stock   D. Loan stock

22. Which of the following attracts a fixed rate of interest?
   A. Preferred stock   B. Common stock   C. Dividend D. Debentures

23. Common stockholders do not have right to
   A. elect the board of directors
   B. receive dividend
   C. receive divided at a predetermined rate
   D. vote at annual general meeting

24. Another name for "Bonus share" is
   A. stock dividend   B. right issue   C. dividend cover   D. scrip issue

25. Payment for shares in installments is done by means of
A. invitation   B. subscription   C. calls   D. notice

26. The class of shares of which payment of dividend depends on profit is
A. preferred stock   B. forfeited shares   C. issued shares D. common stock

27. Shares issued to a vendor in payment of business purchased would require a debit to
A. Cash account and credit to share capital account
B. Share capital account and credit to vendor's account
C. Vendor's account and credit to share capital account.
D. Share capital account and credit to cash

28. A debenture holder is
 A. an underwriter   B. a debtor   C. a promoter   D. a creditor

29. A stock as a form of company's capital consist of
A. goods B. units of shares   C. work in progress   D. raw material

30. Any asset which has no realizable value is called
 A. Tangible asset B. Intangible asset   C. Fictitious asset D. Wasting asset

31. Which of the following cannot be regarded as an example of capital reserve?
   A. share premium B. revaluation surplus C. capital redemption reserve
   D. general reserve

32. Which of the following is a fictitious asset?
 A. Goodwill B. patent right C. preliminary expense   D. equipment

33. The two main types of reserves are

A. general reserve and revenue reserve
B. retained earnings and earnings per share
C. revaluation surplus and share premium
D. capital reserve and revenue reserve

34. In a limited company which of the following is shown in the statement of changes in
   equity?
   (i) directors' remuneration (ii) debenture interest (iii) loan stock (iv)dividend paid
   (v) transfers to reserves
   A. (i) and (ii) only B. (i) and (iii) only C. (iv) and (v) only D. (ii) only

35. Smith limited issued 100,000 common stock of $1 each at market value of $3.50 each. The share premium is
   A. $125,000 B. $200,000 C. $25,000 D. $250,000

36. A company has 5% debentures worth $350,000, common stock $1,500,000, and preferred stock $9,000,000. If the company made a profit of $850,000, the debenture interest would be amounted to
   A. $200,000 B. $250,000 C. $25,000 D. $17,500

Use the following information to answer question 37 and 39

The authorized capital of Samopex company is made up of 100,000 2.5% preferred stock $30 each and 150,000 common stock of $10 each. 90% of the common stock have been issued at $15 each and fully paid. All the preferred stock have been issued and fully paid. The directors decided to pay the preferred dividend and recommended common stock dividend of $0.5 per share.

37. What is the amount of preferred dividend payable?
   A. $7,500 B. $25,000 C. $2,500 D. $75,000

38. What is the amount of share premium?
   A. $750,000 B.$ 75,000 C. $675,000 D. $235,000

39. What is the value of common stock capital that will be stated on the statement of financial position?

A. $1,350,000   B.$ 2,025,000   C. $675,000   D.$ 150,000

40. Which of the following is not a purpose for which share premium may be utilized?
A. writing off preliminary expenses
B. issuing fully paid bonus issue
C. providing for a redeemable preference shares
D. Settling petty expenses

41. A class of Preferred stock in which dividend rights are carried forward to next period is called
   A. redeemable preferred stock   B. cumulative preferred stock
   C. irredeemable preferred stock   D. ordinary common stock

Use the following information to answer question 42 to 43

A business whose assets consisted of inventory $1,200,000 and accounts receivable (debtors) $1,100,000   was bought by issuing 5,000,000 common stock of 50 cents each at a premium of 20%.

42. What is the purchase consideration?
A. $3,000,000   B.$ 300,000   C.$ 6,300,000   D. $1,300,000

43. What is the amount of goodwill on the business purchased?
A. $7,500,000   B. $6,200,000   C. $2,500,000   D.$ 700,000

44. A Company issued 18,000 9% Debentures at $98. What is the interest payable on the debentures per annum?
   A. $162,000 B.$ 158,760 C. $178,000 D. $220,000

45. The document that governs the external relationship of a company and defines the extent of its power and range of activities is called......
   A. Prospectus B. Article of Association C. Memorandum of Association
   D. Debenture deed

46. The residual between the total assets and liabilities of a company is

A. Shareholders' fund   B. Capital employed   C. working capital
D. capital reserve

Use the following question to answer question 47 to 48
Pololo Plc has the following balances on 31st December, 2011:

	$
Share Premium Account	15,000
20,000 8% preferred stock of $1 each	20,000
10% debenture	25,000
Current liabilities	15,000
150,000 common stock of $1 each	150,000
General reserves	22,000
Profit and loss account balance	50,000
Assets	297,000

47. The shareholders' fund is
A. $270,000   B. $257,000   C. $225,000   D. $297,000

48. What is the value of capital employed?
A. $233,000   B. $282,000   C. $257,000   D. $297,000

Use the following information to answer questions 49 – 50

Common stock of $0.5 each	$6,000,000
8% preferred stock of $1 each	$2,500,000
Interim dividend paid:	
Common stock	$500,000
Preferred stock	$165,000
Profit for the year	$1,200,000

49. If no profit is to be retained, what are the final dividends of preferred stock and the final dividends of common stock respectively?
    A. $35,000 and $500,000   B. $30,000 and $120,000
    C. $700,000 and $35,000   D. $165,000 and $500,000

50. The final dividend per common stock for the year is
   A. $0.658   B. $0.117   C. $0.042   D. $24

CHAPTER 12

ACCOUNTING RATIOS

1. One of the benefits of using accounting ratio is that they
A. are easy to calculate
B. facilitate decision-making
C. are stipulated by law
D. show errors and frauds.

2. Given

Cost of sales	$250,000
Sales	$320,000

The gross profit mark- up is
   A. 23%   B. 28%   C. 22% D. 15%

Use the following information to answer question 3 to 6.

	$	$
Sales		250,000
Opening stocks	?	
Purchases	100,000	
Less: Closing stocks	80,000	
Cost of sales	?	
Gross profit		?

The gross profit margin for the above information is 25%.

3. Calculate cost of sales.
A. $250,000 B. $187,500 C. $190,000 D. $120,000

4. Compute gross profit
A. $80,000 B. $62,500 C. $46,875 D. $18,000

5. Compute Gross profit mark-up

A. 25% B. 30% C. 22.22% D. 33.33%

6. Calculate the opening stock.
   A. $167,500 B.$ 67,500 C. $187,500 D. $100,000

7. Calculate stock turnover rate
   A. 1.5times B. 2.5times C. 3times D. 6times

Use the following to answer questions 5 to 7

	$
Net profit	80,000
Total Assets	600,000
Current Liabilities	180,000
Current Assets	310,000

8. The current ratio is
   A. 1.72 : 1 B. 0.6 : 1 C. 1:2 D. 7.2 : 1

9. The capital employed is
   A. $150,000 B. $420,000 C. $310,000 D. $130,000

10. The return on capital employed is
    A. 61.54% B. 25.8% C.19.05% D. 1.72%

11. A low current asset ratio in a business indicates that the business is
    A. Able to use its resources efficiently
    B. Unable to pay its short-term bills as at when due
    C. Able to meets its short-term loan
    D. Keeping its assets

12. Which of the following best measure the ability of a firm to meet its short-term financial obligation?
    A. Current ratio B. stock turn over C. acid test ratio D. creditor payment period

Use the following information to answer question 13 – 17

The balance sheet extract of Jane Limited is given as follows:

	2009	2008
	$'000	$'000
Cash	1,130	-
Investment (marketable security)	860	750
Accounts receivable	5,030	5,350
Inventory	7,900	6,500
	14,920	12,600
Trade Creditors	-7,730	-7,150
Bank overdraft		-360
	7,190	5,090

13. Compute current ratio for the year 2009 and 2008 respectively.

   A. 1.93 and 1.68 B.1 and 1.2 C.0.9 and 1.9 D.1.68 and 1.93

14. Compute quick ratio for the year 2009 and 2008 respectively.
   A.0.98 and 1 B. 1.5 and 2 C.1 and 2 D. 0.91 and 0.81

15. Compute acid test ratio for year 2009.
   A.0.91: 1 B. 0.81:1 C. 1 : 0.8 D. 2 : 1

16. Calculate working capital for year 2009 and 2008 respectively.
   A. $660 and $750 B.$ 7,730 and $7,510 C. $7,190 and $5,090
   D. $5,090 and $7,190

17. Compute cash ratio for year 2009.
   A. 0.4: 1 B.1.2:1 C. 2: 1 D. 0.26: 1

18. The price-earnings ratio for a company with earnings per share of $4.32 is 11. If the total number of shares in issue is 60,000, what is the total market value of the share?
   A. $2,851,200 B. $2,852,100 C. $23,564 D. $259,200

19. The ratio expressing the relationship between debt capital and Equity holders' funds is called
    A. debt ratio B. interest cover C. proprietor ratio D. gearing ratio

20. Which of the following will be excluded from the calculation of acid test ratio?
    A. cash at hand B. bank balance C. inventory D. accounts receivable

Use the following information to answer question 20 to 24. J.J. Ltd., during the current accounting period, had sales (all on credit) of $415,000 and cost of goods sold of $262,500. At the beginning of the year, its Accounts Receivable were $40,000 and its inventory was $50,000. At the end of the year, its Accounts Receivable were $43,000 and its inventory was $55,000.

21. Compute accounts receivable collection period
    A. 42 days B. 37 days C. 27 days D.40 days

22. Compute accounts receivable turnover
    A. 9 times B.11 times C. 13 days D. 10 times

23. Stock turnover rate is
    A. 5 times B. 7 times C. 73 times D. 1825days

24. Stock turnover period is
    A. 37days B. 73 days C. 83 days D.73 times

25. Victory company Ltd. has a debt-to-equity ratio of 1.9 compared with the industry average of 1.5. This means that the company
    A. has less liquidity than other firm
    B. has higher credit worthiness than the industrial average
    C. Will be able to meet its financial obligation earlier than other firms in the industry
    D. has greater financial risk than other firms in the industry

Use the following information to answer questions 26 to 31.

The following were extracted from the books of Jendo International Ltd.

	2014	2013
	$	$
Net profit after taxation	24,960	21,940
Dividend proposed	-12,000	-11,500
Retained profit	12,960	10,440

An extract from the statement of financial position (balance sheet) as at 31st December, 2014

	2014	2013
	$	$
Common stock of $1 each	50,000	42,000
Share premium	18,000	18,000
Capital reserves	22,000	22,000
Revenue reserves	32,000	25,000
	122,000	107,000
Non-current liabilities		
10% debenture	15,000	15,000
	137,000	122,000

NOTE: The market price of the company's share has been fairly stable at $4 per share.
    Taxation for year 2014 and 2013 were $10,697 and $9,403 respectively.

26. Calculate earning per share for the year 2014 and 2013 respectively from the above information
    A. $0.22 and $1.67   B. $0.499 and $0.522   C. $1.2 and $2.1

27. Compute dividend per share for year 2014 and 2013 respectively
    A. $0.24 and $0.274   B. $0.50 and $0.52   C. $0.274 and $0.24
    D.$2 and $1.5

28. Compute dividend cover for year 2014 and year 2013 respectively
A. 3.5times and 2.5times B. 0.48times and 0.53times
C. 2.08 times and 1.91times D. 3times and 2times

29. Compute dividend yield for year 2014 and year 2013 respectively
A. 6% and 6.85% B. 20% and 30%
C. 14% and 12% D. 0.3times and 2.3times

30. Calculate earnings yield for year 2013
A. 21.1% B. 13.05% C. 22% D. 18%

31. Calculate return on capital employed for year 2013
A. 22% B. 23% C. 20.51% D. 26.92%

32. Compute gearing ratio for the year 2014
A. 2% B.112% C. 12% D. 14%

33. Which of the following is an effect of highly geared company?
A. It encourages employees
B. It discourages employees
C. It discourages creditors and investors
D. It boosts the income

34. The market price of PTV Company's ordinary shares increase from $4 to $6. Earning per share remained constant. The company's price-earnings ratio would
A. decrease B. be constant C. increase D. non of the above

35. Somopex & company ltd. has a current ratio of 1.2 : 1 The current ratio later decreased to 1:1. Which of the following is a cause of the decrease?
A. payment of accounts payable
B. collection of accounts receivable
C. additional bad debt written off
D. Purchase of inventory for cash

36. The only assets possessed by a company are inventory $2,500,000, cash at bank $250,000, and receivables $1,200,000. The current ratio of the company is 2:1. What is the quick ratio?
A. 0.67: 1   B. 0.73:1   C. 0.33:1   D. 2:1

37. Which of the following is a formula for calculating interest cover?
A. profit before interest and tax divided by interest
B. profit minus interest plus tax divided by interest
C. Interest divided by profit plus interest and tax
D. Interest divided by Net profit

38. Which of the following ratio is not used in measuring short term solvency and liquidity of a company?
A. cash ratio   B. current ratio   C. quick ratio   D. Net cash flow ratio

39. Which of the following is not a ratio for measuring long-term solvency of a company?
A. debt ratio   B. gearing ratio   C. interest cover   D. dividend cover

40. Earnings yield is an example of which ratio?
A. Shareholders Investment ratio   B. solvency ratio   C. liquidity ratio   D. activity ratio

CHAPTER 13

JOINT VENTURE

1. A temporary arrangement where two or more businesses pooled their economic resources together to attain a specific task is called
A. Partnership
B. Economic entity
C. Amalgamation
D. Joint Venture
E. Merger

2. When two or more businesses join together for a particular business venture, and do not form a particular business entity, they have entered into a ....
A. Business plan
B. Partnership accounts
C. Memo
D. Joint venture

3. **True** or **False**
Separate set of books or separate bank accounts are kept for smaller joint ventures.

4. **True** or **False**
For large scale or long-term joint ventures, a separate bank account and separate set of books are kept.

Use the following information to answer questions 5 to 7.

Brown and Green are in the same state, but different towns. They enter into a joint venture. Brown is to supply the goods and pay some of the expenses. Green is to sell the goods and receive the cash, and pay the remainder of the expenses. Profits are to be shared equally.
Details of the transactions are as follows:

	$
Brown supplied the goods costing	3,600

Brown paid wages	400
Brown paid for storage expenses	320
Green paid transport expenses	240
Green paid selling expenses	640
Green received cash from sales of all the goods	6,400

5. What is the share of profit or loss of Brown and Green respectively?
A. $600; $600
B. $300; $300
C. $450; $150
D. $ 200;$400

6. Which of the following is correct?
A. Brown is indebted to Green
B. Green is indebted to Brown
C. Green is the owner of the business
D. Brown is the owner of the business

7. How much will be settled by Green to Brown?
A. $4,920
B. $2,094
C. $5,900
D. $2,460

8. An account drawn up only to find out the shares of net profit or loss of each party to the joint venture is called ....
A. Joint Venture
B. Appropriation accounts
C. Memorandum joint venture account
D. Statements of changes in equity

APPENDICES

SOLUTIONS

SOLUTION TO ACCOUNTING EQUATION MCQS

1) The correct answer is B. Mortgage of office building, inventory and computers.

Mortgage of office building is a liability and cannot be classified as an asset.
Inventory is an asset and cannot be classified as a liability.
Computers are assets and cannot be classified as liabilities.

2) The correct answer is C. $5,000.
This question can be solved using accounting equation. The equation is:

Asset = Capital + Liability
$5,000 = $4,350 +$650

It can be seen from the above that out of the cash deposited to bank, $4,350 belongs to C. Palic and $650 was borrowed from friends. If these two values are added together, we will get the total asset which is $5,000.

3) The correct answer is B. $1,840.
The capital at the beginning of year 2013 will be:
    Capital at February 1, 2012 – Net loss
    = $1,900 – $60
    = $1,840
Note: Net loss is always deducted from the opening capital to get the closing capital because net loss has a negative value.

4) The correct answer is D) $3,519
The capital at January 1, 2011 =

=January 1, 2010 + Net loss
= $2,500 + $1,019
= $ 3,519

Note: Net profit is always added to opening capital because it is a positive figure.

5) The correct answer is C).
    Payment of expenses will definitely reduce assets. You can either pay by cash or bank. Bank and cash are assets from which expenses could be paid from. Either of these two will be reduced whenever there is a payment.

6) The right answer is C) decreases assets and decreases liabilities.
    Payment of accounts payable will reduce asset. It will also reduce liability because accounts payable is a liability and once is paid for, it reduces.

Look at the accounting equation here:

Asset = Capital + Liability

The asset reduces by the amount paid from asset (cash or bank) and liability also reduces by the amount of the liability (accounts payable) that was paid.

7) The correct answer is A)
The solution can also be picked from the above equation. If capital increases, assets must also increase. This will be more explained in double entry principles of accounts.

8) The correct answer is D)
    Asset = Capital + Liability

9) The correct answer is A)

10) The correct answer is C) principles of double entry book-keeping

11) This question can be solved by a basic accounting equation

ASSETS	$
Building	?
Cash	15,000
Plant and Machinery	300,000
Debtors	60,000

LIABILITIES	$
Loan	250,000
Creditors	25,000
	275000

ASSETS = CAPITAL + LIABILITY

Building + $375,000 = $500,000 + $275,000
Building + $375,000 = $775,000
Building = $775,000 - $375,000
= $400,000

The correct answer is C) $400,000

12) The correct answer is D) Bank overdraft

13) The correct answer is D) Tax owed
14) The correct answer is C) $685,000
The accounting equation can be used to solve this question.
Assets = Capital +Liabilities

Owner's Equity = Assets – Liabilities

Assets	$
Account receivable	20,000
Machinery	200,000

Land and building	520,000
	740,000

Liabilities	$
Mortgage loan	40,000
Account payable	15,000
	55,000

Owner's Equity = $740,000 – $55,000
       = $685,000

15) The answer is D) $80,000
The basic accounting equation can be used to solve this equation.

Assets = Capital + Liabilities
Assets = $65,000 +$15,000
       = $ 80,000

16) A) Increase in asset and increase in capital
17) B) Asset
18) B) credit balance
19) The answer is C)
       Assets = Liabilities + Owner's equity+ Revenue – Expenses – Owner's drawings

20. B	26. B	32. D	38. B
21. C	27. D	33. C	39. D
22. C	28. B	34. A	40. D
23. A	29. C	35. C	
24. B	30. C	36. D	
25. B	31. D	37. C	

SOLUTION TO SOURCE DOCUMENTS AND BOOKS OF ACCOUNTS

1. C	21. A	41. D
2. C	22. C	42. D
3. C	23. D	43. C

4. D	24. C	44. D
5. D	25. B	45. D
6. D	26. D	46. C
7. B	27. D	47. D
8. D	28. C	48. C
9. A	29. D	49. C
10. D	30. C	50. A
11. D	31. C	
12. B	32. C	
13. B	33. C	
14. B	34. C	
15. D	35. A	
16. C	36. C	
17. C	37. D	
18. B	38. C	
19. B	39. C	
20. B	40. A	

WORKINGS

49. $(250,000 \times 75\%)90\% = \$168,750$

50. $6 \times \$24 - 6 \times \$24 \times 1/3 = \$96$

SOLUTION TO ACCOUNTING CONCEPTS AND CONVENTIONS

1	D	21	B
2	D	22	B
3	C	23	C

4	D	24	A
5	B	25	D
6	B	26	D
7	D	27	D
8	D	28	D
9	B	29	B
10	B	30	D
11	A	31	D
12	C	32	D
13	D	33	B
14	B	34	A
15	B	35	D
16	C	36	B
17	D	37	C
18	A	38	D
19	A	39	D
20	C	40	C

SOLUTION TO ADJUSTMENTS TO ACCOUNTS

1. D	21. D
2. C	22. C
3. B	23. D

4. B	24. B
5. B	25. C
6. B	26. D
7. B	27. B
8. C	28. A
9. C	29. C
10. C	30. B
11. B	31. A
12. D	32. C
13. A	33. A
14. D	34. A
15. A	35. C
16. D	36. D
17. C	37. C
18. D	38. B
19. C	39. D
20. C	40. A

WOKINGS

1. $2,500/15 \times 10 = \$1,666.67$
2. $\$2,500 - \$1,666.67 = \$833.33$. This is an advance payment (January 2008 to May,2008).
   Advance payment is a current asset.

3. Rent for the current year

	$
Cash paid for during the year	6,000
Less rent owing b/d	-600
Add rent owing c/d	800
Rent for the current year	6,200

27. $66,000 \times 2\% = \$1,320$

28. $(66,000 - 1,320) \times 5\% = \$3,234$

33. Mark up = 1/4

Margin = 1/4+1 = 1/5 or 20%

Mark up is multiplied by cost price to get gross profit while margin is multiplied by selling price to get gross profit.

Therefore, the correct answer is 20% of selling price

34. Mark up = profit /cost price

$$= \frac{24,000 - 18,000}{18,000}$$

$$= 33 \, ^1/3$$

35. Accounts Receivable to be shown in the statement of financial position

	$
Accounts receivable	
31/5/2014	525,110
Less: Bad debts for the year	(41,000)
	484,110
Less: Allowance for doubtful	
debts (484,110 × 5%)	(24,205.5)
	459,904.5

36.

Allowance for bad and doubtful debts Accounts

	$		$
		Balance b/d	12,500
Balance c/d	24,206	Income(P&L)	11,706
	24,206		24,206
		Balance b/d	24,206

37.

Rates Accounts

	$		$
Balance b/d	500	P&L	1,400

Cash	1,500	Balance c/d	600
	2,000		2,000
Balance b/d	600		

38.

Rent Accounts

	$		$
Cash	2,000	Balance b/d	1,000
Balance c/d	500	P&L	1,500
	2,500		2,500
		Balance b/d	500

39.

Interest on loan Accounts

	$		$
Cash	350	Balance b/d	1,200
Balance c/d	1,400	Income(P&L)	550
	1,750		1,750
		Balance b/d	1,400

40.

Wages Accounts

	$		$
Cash	72,500	Balance b/d	1,000
Balance c/d	750	P&L	72,250
	73,250		73,250
		Balance b/d	750

SOLUTION TO BANK RECONCILIATION

1. B	11. B	21. B	31. D
2. A	12. D	22. B	32. C
3. D	13. A	23. A	33. D
4. C	14. B	24. C	34. A
5. D	15. B	25. C	35. B
6. C	16. B	26. D	36. A
7. C	17. A	27. C	37. D
8. C	18. D	28. B	38. D
9. C	19. A	29. D	39. D
10. C	20. B	30. C	40. A

WORKINGS

12.
   $4 \times \$20,000 = \$80,000$
This is an example of a standing order.

14.   Bank reconciliation statement

	$	$
Balance as per adjusted cash book		4,500
Add: Unpresented checks		3,000
		7,500
Less: Uncredited checks	(2,500)	
Less:Cash in transit	(1,000)	(3,500)
Balance as per bank statement		4,000

16.

Adjusted cash book

	$		$
Undercast debit	10,000	Balance b/d	16,000
Balance c/d	11,600	Check paid	4,000
		Bank commission	1,600
	21,600		21,600
		Balance b/d	11,600

17.

Bank Reconciliation Statement	$
Balance as per adjusted cash book	-11,600
Add: Unpresented check	28,800
Less: Uncredited check	-5,200
Balance as per bank statement	12,000

19.

	$
Balance as per bank statement	-16,600
Add: uncredited check	32,000
	15,400

29.

Adjusted Cash Book

	$		$
		Balance b/d	3,030
		Standing order	980
Balance c/d	4,540	Bank Charges	530
	4,540		4,540
		Balance b/d	4,540

30.

Adjusted Cash Book

	$		$
Balance b/d	16,000	Check paid	4,000
Undercast	10,000	Bank commission	1,600
		Balance c/d	20,400
	26,000		26,000
Balance b/d	20,400		

31.

Bank Reconciliation Statement	$
Balance as per Adjusted cash book	20,400
Add: Unpresented check	28,800
	49,200
Less: Uncredited check	-5,200
Balance as per bank statement	44,000

34.

Adjusted cash book

	$
Balance b/f	360,000
Check issued in error (72,000 × 2)	-144,000
	216,000
Bank charges	-74,000
Adjusted cash book	142,000

39.

	$
Cash book (bank balance)	5,200
Less check paid: (2,000 – 400) - ($2,000- 400)10%	(1,440)
Add check deposited	475
Balance at bank at the end of the month	4,235

40.

Adjusted cash book as at 31st December, 2009.

	$
Balance b/d	3,250
Bank charges	-64
Dishonored check	<u>-295</u>
	2,891

SOLUTION TO DEPRECIATION ACCOUNTS

1. A	21. B	41. D
2. B	22. A	42. D
3. D	23. C	43. D
4. B	24. B	44. B
5. C	25. B	45. C
6. D	26. B	
7. D	27. B	
8. C	28. D	
9. C	29. C	
10. B	30. B	
11. C	31. B	
12. B	32. A	
13. B	33. B	
14. B	34. C	
15. B	35. C	
16. B	36. B	
17. C	37. C	
18. D	38. D	
19. C	39. C	
20. B	40. C	

WORKINGS

11. Annual depreciation

$$= \frac{24,000 - 800}{8}$$

$$= \$2,900$$

12. $6 \times \$2,900 = \$17,400$

13.

	$
Year 1 Cost	24,000
Less: Depreciation (25% ×24,000)	-6,000
Year 2 Balance	18,000
Less : Depreciation (25% × 18,000)	-4,500
	13,500

15.

Disposal of asset a/c

	$		$
		Depreciation	36,000
		Bank	60,000
Cost	100,000	Loss	4,000
	100,000		100,000

16.

	$
Year 1 Cost	1,500,000
Year 1 Depreciation (20%×1,500,000)	-300,000
Book value after year 1	1,200,000
Year 2 Depreciation(20%×1,200,000)	-240,000
Book value after year 2	960,000

20. $17,000 - (4,000 \times 4) = \$1,000$

21. $3.5 \times 20\% \times \$120,000 = \$84,000$

22.

	$
Sales value	31,500
Accumulated depreciation	<u>84,000</u>
	115,500
Less cost	<u>-120,000</u>
Loss	-4,500

23.

	$
Cost	120,000
Accumulated depreciation	<u>-84,000</u>
Net Book Value	36,000

24. $= 120,000 + 11,000 + 5,500$
    $= \$136,500$

25.

	$
Year 1 cost	136,500
Depreciation (20%×136,500)	<u>-27,300</u>
Year 2 Balance	109,200
Depreciation (20%×109,200)	21,840

26. $\dfrac{136,500 - 6,000}{5} = \$26,100$

31. $= 10,000 + 1,500 + 1,800$
    $= \$13,300$

32.

	$
Sales Proceeds	5,000
Accumulated depreciation	4,788
	9,788
Less: Cost	(13,300)
Net loss	-3,512

33.

	$
Cost	13,300
Less: accumulated depreciation	-4,788
Net book value	8,512

36.

	$
Disposal of non- current asset	600,000
Closing balance	1,500,000
	2,100,000
Less: Additional Asset	-92,000
Opening balance	2,008,000

37.

	$
Depreciation on asset disposed	110,000

Depreciation at end of the year	200,000
	310,000
Less: Depreciation at beginning	-250,000
Depreciation expenses charged	60,000

43.

$$\frac{\$420,000 - \$15,000}{n} = \$84,000$$

$$n = \frac{\$405,000}{\$84,000}$$

$$n = 4.82 \text{ years}$$

$$n = 5 \text{ years}$$

44.

Depreciation for year 1

$$\frac{420,000}{5} = \$84,000$$

Percentage of depreciation

$$\$420,000 \times y/100 = \$84,000$$

$$y = \frac{\$8,400,000}{\$420,000} = 20$$

$$y = 20\%$$

45.

	$
	$
Year 1, Cost	420,000
Year 1, Depreciation	-84,000
Year 2, Balance b/d	336,000
Year 2, Depreciation	-67,200
Year 3, Balance b/d	268,800
Year 3, Depreciation	-53,760
	215,040

SOLUTIONS TO CONTROL ACCOUNTS

1. C	11. B	21. D	31. C
2. B	12. A	22. B	32. C
3. D	13. A	23. D	33. A
4. A	14. B	24. C	34. C
5. A	15. C	25. D	35. C
6. D	16. B	26. C	36. B
7. D	17. D	27. C	37. A
8. B	18. B	28. A	38. B
9. A	19. C	29. B	39. C
10. B	20. C	30. C	40. D

WORKINGS

4.

Purchases Ledger Control Accounts

	$		$
Discounts received	120	Balance b/d	270
Bank	450	Purchases	800
Balance c/d	500		
	1,070		1,070
		Balance b/d	500

The balance b/d is $270. It is the difference between the Dr. and Cr. side above.

12. Net sales = Sales – Return inwards
$$= 21,410 – 742$$
$$= \$20,668$$

18.

Purchases Ledger Control Accounts

	$		$

Bank	906,000	Balance b/d	609,000
Balance		Credit	
c/d	96,000	purchases	393,000
	1,002,000		1,002,000
		Balance b/d	96,000

20.

Purchases Ledger Control Accounts

	$		$
Cash	37,000	Balance b/d	6,000
Balance c/d	10,500	Purchases	41,500
	47,500		47,500
		Balance b/d	10,500

21. cost of sales:

= opening inventory + purchases – closing inventory

= $4,000+ $41,500 –$6,400= $39,100

28.

Sales Ledger Control Accounts

	$		$
Balance b/d	60,000	Bad debts	6,500
Credit sales	105,000	Set- offs	77,000
		Balance c/d	81,500
	165,000		165,000
Balance b/d	81,500		

29.

Purchases Ledger Control Accounts

	$		$
Set-offs	77,000	Balance b/d	50,000
Balance c/d	68,000	Credit purchases	95,000
	145,000		145,000
		Balance b/d	68,000

33.

Purchases Ledger Control Accounts

	$		$
Returned outward	1,620	Balance b/d	21,280
Cash discount received	2,696	Purchases	53,824
Cash paid	41,616	Balance c/d	216
Balance c/d	29,388		
	75,320		75,320
Balance b/d	216	Balance b/d	29,388

38.

Purchases Ledger Control Accounts

	$		$
Discount received	15,000	Balance b/d	325,000
Sales ledger contra	175,000	Credit purchases	1,000,000
Bank	930,000		
Balance c/d	205,000		
	1,325,000		1,325,000
		Balance b/d	205,000

SOLUTION TO NON-PROFIT MAKING ORGANIZATIONS

1. D	11. C	21. B	31. B
2. C	12. C	22. B	32. D
3. C	13. C	23. D	33. A
4. B	14. B	24. D	34. C
5. C	15. A	25. A	35. D
6. B	16. C	26. D	36. D
7. D	17. C	27. C	37. C
8. A	18. B	28. B	38. D
9. A	19. B	29. B	39. A
10. B	20. B	30. C	40. C

WORKINGS

12.
$6,000×85% = $5,100

14.

Subscription A/C

	$		$
Owing b/d	3,000	Bank	25,000
Income &			
Expenditure	23,500	Owing c/d	1,500
	26,500		26,500
Owing b/d	1,500		

18.

Subscription Accounts

	$		$
Owing b/d	80	Advance b/d	25
Income &			
Expenditure	2,570	Bank	2,560
		Balance c/d	65
	2650		2650
Balance c/d	65		

19.

The current liability is zero because none of the members paid subscription in advance at the end of the accounting period to the club.

22.

	$	$
Furniture		500,000
Sport kit		800,000
Club house		750,000
Subscription owing		90,000
		2,140,000
Less:		
Bar creditors	312,000	
Subscription prepaid	20,000	
	332,000	-332,000
Accumulated funds		1,808,000

24.

Statement of affairs as at 1st Jan. 2009

	$	$
Equipment		120,000
Rent		600
Subscription in arrears		3000
Cash		2,000
		125,600
Less:		
Rent (accrual)	400	
Subscription in advance	2,600	-3,000
Accumulated funds		122,600

26.

Subscription Accounts for the year ended 31st Dec. 2009

	$		$
In arrears b/d	3,000	In advance b/d	2,600
In advance c/d	1,600	Bank	30,000
Income & Expenditure	30,000	In arrears	2,000
	34,600		34,600

27.

$$3,000 + 600 - 800 = \$2,800$$

28.

$$30\% \times 60,000 = \$18,000$$

29.

$$\$95,000 - \$28,000 - \$10,000 - \$3,000 = \$36,000$$

SOLUTION TO MANUFACTURING ACCOUNTS

1. D	11. A	21. A
2. A	12. B	22. B
3. D	13. C	23. A
4. D	14. C	24. C
5. B	15. B	25. A
6. C	16. C	26. B
7. C	17. B	27. A
8. A	18. A	28. A
9. B	19. B	29. D
10. B	20. C	30. D

WORKINGS

2. Gross profit = $15/100 \times 182,000 = \$27,300$

3.

	$
Gross profit	27,300
Salary	-28,000
Selling and distribution	-16,000
Net loss	16,700

Answers for question 8 to 11 can be picked from the following:

Manufacturing accounts

	$	$
Opening raw material	16,000	
Raw material purchased	29,000	
	45,000	45,000
Closing stock of raw materials		14,700
Raw material consumed		30,300
Direct labor	8,000	8,000
Prime cost		38,300
Factory overhead		
Electricity	5,000	
Supervisory salary	10,000	
Depreciation of plant	3,000	
Factory overhead cost	18,000	18,000
Cost of production		56,300

Trading accounts

	$	$
Sales		110,000
Less cost of sales:		
Cost of production	56,300	
Less: closing stock	-4,500	
		-51,800
Gross profit		58,200

17.

	$
Prime cost	137,500
Indirect manufacturing cost	66,400
Add: work-in-progress at start	4,500
	208,400
Less: work-in-progress at end	-5,200
Production cost	203,200

19 to 23

Manufacturing accounts for the year ended December 31, 2004

	$	$
	$	$
Opening raw material		9,000
Purchases(raw material)	58,000	
Carriage Inward	2,400	
	60,400	60,400
Raw material available for production		69,400
Closing raw material		- 11,000
Cost of raw material consumed		58,400
Direct wages	68,000	
Royalties	1,000	
	69,000	69,000
Prime cost		127,400
Factory Overhead		
Indirect wages	21,600	
Rent	36,000	
Insurance	6,000	
Factory overhead	63,600	63,600
		191,000
Work-in-progress at start		7,500

	198,500
Work-in-progress at end	-13,500
Cost of goods manufactured	185,000

27.

		$
31st Dec. 2009	Raw materials	200,000
31st Dec. 2009	Work-in-progress	85,000
31st Dec. 2009	Finished goods	68,000
	Inventory	353,000

28.

	$
Total production cost	520,000
Less factory overhead cost	(210,000)
Prime cost	310,000

29.

	$
Prime cost	116,000
Indirect manufacturing cost	68,000
	184,000
Less closing work-in-progress	(38,000)

Total manufacturing cost	146,000

SOLUTION TO PARTNERSHIP ACCOUNTS

1. D	21. A	41. C
2. D	22. D	42. D
3. C	23. B	43. D
4. B	24. B	44. C
5. D	25. B	45. C
6. B	26. C	46. D
7. C	27. B	47. B
8. B	28. B	48. C
9. D	29. B	49. B
10. D	30. B	50. C
11. C	31. C	
12. C	32. C	
13. A	33. B	
14. C	34. A	
15. B	35. A	
16. B	36. A	
17. A	37. D	
18. B	38. C	
19. C	39. C	
20. B	40. C	

WORKINGS

10.
Interest on capital:

			$
		× 12%	
John	30,000	=	3,600
		× 12%	
Audu	50,000	=	6,000
			9,600

11.

	$	$
Net profit		58,000
Less: Salary		
John	12,000	
Audu	16,000	
		(28,000)
		30,000
Less: Interest on capital		
John	3,600	
Audu	6,000	
		(9,600)
Profit available		20,400

12. John $(40\% \times 20{,}400) = \$8{,}160$

13. Audu $(60\% \times 20{,}400) = \$12{,}240$

16 to 19

Profit and Loss appropriation accounts

	$	$
Net profit		14,000
Add: interest on drawings		
Clem($10\% \times 5{,}000$)	500	
Smith ($10\% \times 7{,}000$)	700	1,200
		15,200
Less: Interest on capital		

Clem (5% × 40,000)   2,000

Smith (5% × 20,00)   1,000   -3,000

Available profit   12,200

Share of profit:

Clem (3/5 × 12,200)   7,320

Smith (2/5 × 12,200)   4,880

20 & 21

Partnership current Accounts

	Clem $	smith $		clem $	smith $
Interest			Profit b/d	7,320	4,880
on drawings	500	700	Interest on capital	2,000	1,000
Drawings	5,000	7,000			
Balance c/d	3,820		Balance c/d		1,820
	9,320	7,700		9,320	7,700

25. Paul's share of profit:
= ½ × $30,000
= $15,000

26. John's share of profit:
= ½× $30,000
= $15,000

Note: Where there is no partnership agreement, provisions of partnership Act 1890 should be applied. It states that profit should be shared equally and loan brought into the partnership business by any partner attracts 5% interest.

27. 5% × 15,000 = $750.

Note: Where there is no partnership agreement, any additional money introduced by any partner in the partnership business attracts 5% interest rate.

28. & 29.

Partners' current accounts

	J. Smith	P. Lucia		J. Smith	P. Lucia
	$	$		$	$
Drawings	3,000	3,000	Balance b/d	8,000	12,000
Balance c/d	14,000	14,000	share of profit	9,000	5,000
	17,000	17,000		17,000	17,000

30. $\dfrac{9,000}{5,000}$: $\dfrac{5000}{5,000}$

1.8 : 1

40.

Partnership Dissolution Accounts

Cost of Assets:	$	Bank:	$
Building	100,000	Building and Motor vehicle	140,000
Motor vehicle	50,000		
Cost of dissolution	3,000	Balance c/d	13,000
	153,000		153000

42. The old partners will share the remaining profit after the deduction of the new partner's share.

$1 - 1/4 = 3/4$

Old partner

Partner A : $3/4 \times 3/5 = 9/20$

Partner B: $3/4 \times 2/5 = 6/20$

New partner

$1/4 \times 5/5 = 5/20$

New profit sharing ratio 9:6:5

44. $\dfrac{\$60,000 + \$80,000}{4} = \$35,000$

SOLUTION TO COMPANY'S ACCOUNTS

1. D	21. C	41. B
2. C	22. D	42. A
3. D	23. C	43. D
4. C	24. D	44. A
5. C	25. C	45. C
6. C	26. D	46. A
7. B	27. C	47. B
8. B	28. D	48. B
9. B	29. B	49. A
10. B	30. C	50. C
11. B	31. D	
12. B	32. C	
13. D	33. D	
14. B	34. C	

15. D	35. D
16. D	36. D
17. B	37. D
18. B	38. C
19. B	39. A
20. B	40. D

15. Share split is an intentional reduction in the par value of a unit of common stock by increasing the number of shares.

Nominal value of each share:

$$= \frac{\$1 \times 100\text{million shares}}{200 \text{ million shares}}$$

$$= \$0.5$$

16. Issued share $= 160$ million shares $\times \$0.5$
$$= \$80\text{millions}$$

36.
Debenture interest $= 5\% \times \$350,000$
$$= \$17,500$$

37. $\frac{2.5}{100} \times 100,000 \times \$30 = \$75,000$

38.
Common stock issued at:
Premium $= 90\% \times 150,000 \times \$15 = \$2,025,000$
Par $\quad = 90\% \times 150,000 \times \$10 = \underline{\$1,350,000}$
Share premium $\qquad\qquad\qquad\qquad\quad \$675,000$

39. $1,350,000 will be stated in the statement of financial position because it is the par value.

42.
Purchase consideration:

	$
Nominal value of shares:	
(50cents/100×5,000,000)	2,500,000
Share premium :	
(20/100× 50cents/100 ×5,000,000)	500,000
	3,000,000
Less :	
Inventory	-1,200,000
Accounts receivable	-1,100,000
Purchase consideration	700,000

44.
$18,000 \times 9/100 \times \$100 = \$162,000$

NOTE: The par value of a debenture is often in $100 or $1,000 depending on each state.

47.

	$
Total assets	297,000
Less: Debentures	-25,000
Current liabilities	-15,000
Shareholders' funds	257,000

NOTE:
Shareholders' funds = Total assets – Total liabilities

OR.

$

Share Premium Account	15,000
20,000 8% preferred stock of $1 each	20,000
150,000 common stock of $1 each	150,000
General reserves	22,000
Profit and loss account balance	50,000
Shareholders' funds	257,000

48.

	$
Total assets	297,000
Less current liabilities	(15,000)
Capital employed	282,000

49.
Final dividend of preferred stocks:

	$
Preferred dividend (8/100 × 2,500,000)	200,000
Less interim dividend	(165,000)
Final preferred dividend	35,000

Final dividends of common stocks:

	$
Profit for the year	1,200,000
Less: total preferred dividend	(200,000)
Available profit	1,000,000
Less interim dividend (common stock)	(500,000)
Final dividend (common stock)	500,000

50.

$$\text{Number of shares} = \frac{\$6,000,000}{\$0.5}$$
$$= 12,000,000$$

Final dividend per ordinary share:

$$= \frac{\$500,000}{12,000,000}$$

$$= \$0.042$$

SOLUTION TO ACCOUNTING RATIOS

1. B	11. B	21. B	31. D
2. B	12. C	22. D	32. C
3. B	13. A	23. A	33. C
4. B	14. D	24. B	34. C
5. D	15. A	25. D	35. C
6. A	16. C	26. B	36. B
7. A	17. D	27. A	37. A
8. A	18. A	28. C	38. D
9. B	19. D	29. A	39. D
10. C	20. C	30. B	40. A

WORKINGS

2.
$320,000 - $250,000 = $70,000

Gross Profit mark-up:
= Gross profit/ Cost of sales
= $70,000/$250,000 × 100%
= 28%

3.
Gross profit = 25/100×250,000 = $62,500

Cost of sales = Sales – Gross profit
= $250,000 – $62,500
= $187,500

5.
Gross profit mark-up:

= $62,500/$187,500 × 100
= 33.33%

7. Stock turnover rate
= cost of sales/Average stock
= $187,500/$123,750
= 1.5 times

8. Current ratio = current asset/ current liability

= $310,000/$180,000

= 1.72:1

9. Capital employed = Total assets – Current liabilities
= $600,000 – $180,000
= $420,000

10. Return on capital employed:

$$= \text{Net profit/ Capital employed} \times 100\%$$

$$= \$80,000/\$420,000 \times 100\%$$

$$= 19.05\%$$

14. Quick ratio = (Current assets - inventory)/ Current liability

2009

Quick ratio = $(14,920 – 7,900)/ $ 7,190

$$= 0.98$$

2008

Quick ratio = $(12,600-6,500)/$7,510

$$= 0.81$$

15. Acid test ratio is the same as quick ratio (0.98: 1)

16. Working capital = Current Assets – Current Liabilities

17. Cash ratio = (cash + cash equivalent)/ current Asset

$$= \$(1,130 + 860)/ \$7,730$$

$$= 0.26:1$$

18. Price-earnings ratio = MPS/ EPS

MPS/$ 4.32   = $11

MPS = $47.52

Total market value of the share:

= $47.52×60,000
= $2,851,200

NOTE:
MPS = Market price per share,
EPS = Earning per share

21. ARCP =   AVAR/ SALES × 365days

$$= \frac{\$(40{,}000 + 43{,}000)/2}{\$415{,}000} \times 365days$$

= 37days

NOTE: ARCP = Accounts Receivable Collection Period
        AVR = Average Accounts Receivable

22. Accounts receivable turnover

= Sales/ AVAR

= $415,000/$41,500

= 10times

23. Stock turnover rate = COS/ AVS

$$= \$262,500/\$(50,000 + 55,000)/2$$

$$= 5 \text{ times}$$

NOTE:

COS = Cost of sales,

AVS =Average stock

24. Stock turnover period = AVS/ COS × 365 days

$$= \$\frac{(50,000 + 55,000)/2}{\$262,500}$$

$$= 73 \text{ days}$$

26.	2014	2013

EPS = NPATP/NCS

EPS =$24,960/50,000   = $21,940/42,000

=$0.499   = $0.522

Note:
EPS = earnings per shares
NPATP = Net profit after tax and preference dividend (preferred stock)
NCS   = Numbers of ordinary shares (common stocks)

Net profit after tax and preference dividend is the profit available to common stockholders.

27.	2014	2013

Dividend per share = Dividend/ Number of ordinary shares

= $12,000/50,000   = $11,500/42,000

= $0.24   = $0.274

28.   2014   2013

Dividend cover = Earnings per share/ Dividend per share

= $0.499/$0.24   = $0.522/$0.274

=2.08times   =1.91times

29.   2014   2013

Dividend yield:

= Dividend per share/ Market price per share ×100%

= $0.24/$4 × 100%   = $0.274/ $4 × 100%

= 6%   = 6.85%

30. Earnings yield for year 2013:

= Earnings per share/ Market price per share × 100%

= $0.522/$4 × 100%

= 13.05%

31. Return on capital employed for the year 2013:

Profit before interest and tax/ Capital employed × 100%

= ($21,940 +$1,500 + $9,403)/$122,000 × 100%

= 26.92%

32. Gearing ratio for year 2014:

= Prior charge capital/ Total equity ×100

= $15,000/$122,000 ×100

= 0.12295 ×100

= 0.12 ×100

= 12%

36. Current assets:
= $2,500,000 +$250,000+$1,200,000
= $3,950,000

Current ratio = Current assets/Current liabilities

Current ratio = 2

Current assets/ Current liabilities = 2/1

$ 3,950,000/ Current Liabilities = 2/1

Current liabilities = $1,975,000

Quick Ratio = ($3,950,000 – $2,500,000)/$1,975,000

= 0.73

= 0.73 : 1

SOLUTION TO JOINT VENTURES ACCOUNTS

1	D
2	D
3	FALSE
4	TRUE
5	A
6	B
7	A
8	C

WORKINGS

Working 5

Memorandum Joint Venture Accounts

	$		$
<u>Brown</u>		<u>Green</u>	
Cost of goods	3,600		
Wages	400		
Storage expenses	320		
<u>Green</u>			
Transport			
Expenses	240		
Selling Expenses	640		

Balance c/d	1,200	cash sales	6,400
	6,400		6,400
Share of profit:		Balance b/d	1,200
Brown	600		
Green	600		
	1,200		1,200

Working 6

In the books of Green

Joint Ventures with Brown Account

	$		$
Transport Expenses	240	Cash sales	6,400
Selling Expenses	640		
Green's profit	600		
Balance c/d	4,920		
	6,400		6,400

REFERENCES

Adelaja, T.O. (2006), Adjustments for Financial Statements, USA, Createspace.

Adelaja, T.O. (2006), Double Entry Bookkeeping and Adjustments, USA, Createspace.

www.accountinghour.com